Series / Number 07-034

COVARIANCE STRUCTURE MODELS

An Introduction to LISREL

J. SCOTT LONG
Washington State University

SAGE PUBLICATIONS
The International Professional Publishers
Newbury Park London New Delhi

Printed in the United States of America

For information address:

SAGE Publications, Inc.
2455 Teller Road
Newbury Park, California 91320

SAGE Publications Ltd.
6 Bonhill Street
London EC2A 4PU
United Kingdom

SAGE Publications India Pvt. Ltd.
M-32 Market
Greater Kailash I
New Delhi 110 048 India

International Standard Book Number 0-8039-2045-8

Library of Congress Catalog Card No. 83-050602

93 94 15 14 13 12 11 10

When citing a professional paper, please use the proper form. Remember to cite the correct Sage University Paper series title and include the paper number. One of the following formats can be adapted (depending on the style manual used):

(1) IVERSEN, GUDMUND R. and NORPOTH, HELMUT (1976) "Analysis of Variance." Sage University Paper series on Quantitative Application in the Social Sciences, 07-001. Beverly Hills and London: Sage Pubns.

OR

(2) Iversen, Gudmund R. and Norpoth, Helmut. 1976. *Analysis of Variance.* Sage University Paper series on Quantitative Applications in the Social Sciences, series no. 07-001. Beverly Hills and London: Sage Pubns.

CONTENTS

Notation

Boldface letters are used to indicate matrices and vectors. For example, **B** indicates that B is a matrix. Dimensions of matrices and vectors are indicated by "$(r \times c)$" for a matrix with r rows and c columns. Subscripts to lower case letters indicate elements of a matrix. For example, the $(i,j)^{th}$ element of **B** is indicated as b_{ij}; the ith element of the vector **x** is indicated as x_i. The symbol "′" indicates the transpose of a matrix; **B′** is the transpose of **B**. The symbol "–1" as a superscript of a matrix indicates the inverse of the matrix; $\mathbf{B}^{-1}$ is the inverse of **B**. "COV" is the covariance operator. If the arguments of the operator are two variables, say x_i and x_j, then $COV(x_i, x_j)$ indicates the covariance between x_i and x_j. If the argument of the covariance operator is a vector, say **x** of dimension $(n \times 1)$, then COV (**x**) is the $(n \times n)$ covariance matrix whose $(i,j)^{th}$ element (for $i \neq j$) is the covariance between x_i and x_j, and whose $(i,i)^{th}$ element is the variance of x_i. Similarly, "COR" is used as the correlation operator. COR (x_i, x_j) indicates the correlation between x_i and x_i. COR(**x**) is the $(n \times n)$ correlation matrix whose $(i,j)^{th}$ element (for $i \neq j$) is the correlation between x_i and x_j, and whose $(i,i)^{th}$ element is one. "E" is the expectation operator. If x_i is a random variable, $E(x_i)$ is the expected value of x_i. If **x** is a vector, then E(**x**) is a vector whose i^{th} element is the expected value of the random variable x_i.

Figures, equations, examples, and tables are numbered sequentially within chapters. Thus, Table 2.3 is the third table in Chapter 2. Examples are also numbered sequentially within chapters. Thus Example 3.2 refers to the second example in Chapter 3. Some examples are developed in several steps throughout a chapter. Thus, if Example 3.2 appears several times in Chapter 3, the reader should realize that it is the development of the same example.

Preface

This monograph presents a statistical model referred to variously as the covariance structure model, the analysis of covariance structures, the linear structural relations model, the moments structure model, latent variable equation systems in structured linear models, and (perhaps most commonly) the LISREL model. "Covariance structure model" is probably the most general term—hence the name of this monograph. Estimating the covariance structure model requires the use of sophisticated software. LISREL, written by Jöreskog and Sörbom, is by far the most commonly used program for estimating the covariance structure model. The importance of LISREL is evidenced by the fact that the term LISREL has come to stand for not only software but also a statistical model and an approach to data analysis. This importance is reflected by the subtitle of the monograph, "An Introduction to LISREL." The monograph is not, however, an introduction to the control cards necessary to use a particular software package.

While many readers may be unfamiliar with the covariance structure model in its full complexity, it is likely that most have already, even if unwittingly, mastered parts of the model, since the covariance structure model consists of two components, each of which is a powerful and well-known statistical technique in its own right. The first component is the confirmatory factor model considered in psychometrics; the second component is the structural equation model considered in econometrics. This monograph is designed to take advantage of a reader's familiarity with one or both of these components.

The reader is assumed to be familiar with the confirmatory factor model and the mathematical tools presented in a companion volume in the Sage Series on Quantitative Applications in the Social Sciences: *Confirmatory Factor Analysis: A Preface to LISREL*. Since results from that volume are referred to frequently, it is designated simply as *CFA*. The reader whose primary interest is in the structural equation model will find our discussion to be particularly useful for the estimation of models with equality constraints and correlated errors across some but not all equations (e.g., panel models).

A full understanding of the covariance structure model requires the application of the model to actual data. Readers are encouraged to replicate the analyses presented in the text, using the data contained in the Appendix. If the results you obtain match those presented in the text, you have a good indication of your understanding. To estimate the covariance structure model it is generally necessary to use software not contained in such packages as the Statistical Package for the Social Sciences (SPSS), the Statistical Analysis System (SAS), and BMDP statistical software. The concluding chapter briefly describes the software that can be used.

A number of people generously gave of their time to comment on various portions of this monograph. I would like to thank Paul Allison, Greg Duncan, Karen Pugliesi, Jay Stewart, Blair Wheaton, Ronald Schoenberg, and two anonymous reviewers. Carol Hickman read several drafts of both *Confirmatory Factor Analysis* and this manuscript. Her comments greatly improved the accuracy and clarity of the final product. Remaining errors and lack of clarity are the result of not heeding the advice of those listed above.

Series Editor's Introduction

Covariance Structure Models (CSM) builds directly on Professor Long's other volume in this series, *Confirmatory Factor Analysis (CFA)*. Readers unfamiliar with the confirmatory model should read the *CFA* volume before undertaking to read this monograph. A good familiarity with the language of factor analysis and of matrices is necessary to appreciate the appeal and value of CSM.

This volume presents the measurement model, followed by the structural equation model, that together comprise the covariance structure model. In Chapter 2 Professor Long discusses the measurement model, building upon his earlier presentation of the confirmatory factor model. For readers who have studied and understood his earlier presentation, this material will be straightforward and will not introduce any really new or difficult material. Adjustments must be made in notation, but they are minor.

In Chapter 3 the structural equation model is introduced. Here, the reader should have some familiarity with a standard econometric presentation of structural equation models. Professor Long presents this model as if all variables were directly observed—i.e., as if the problem of measurement error, introduced in Chapter 2, did not exist. He later relaxes this assumption and weds the measurement and structural equation models, but for pedagogic purposes he chooses to introduce the structural model without reference to the former. This allows him to build separately on two identifiable quantitative traditions: the literature of psychometrics for the measurement model, and the literature of econometrics for the structural equation model. This is sensible, as most readers will no doubt have greater familiarity with one or the other of these traditions. Few will have been exposed in any great depth to both fields.

In a sense, in Chapter 3 of this volume Professor Long parallels his work in the *CFA* volume. He provides detailed discussions of types of structural equation models, and of the topics of identification and estimation in these models. Criteria of goodness of fit are also discussed in some depth.

In Chapter 4 the covariance structure model is presented. For those readers who have worked through the *CFA* volume and Chapter 3 of this volume, Chapter 4 is simply a review. Here the CFA model is adjusted to take into account the structural relations among unmeasured variables, and the structural equation model is adjusted to recognize the prevalence of errors of measurement and the fact that most of our concepts in social science research are not directly observed. The resulting covariance structure model is much more powerful in what it can do, and in the realism of its assumptions, than is either of its components. There are, to be sure, potential costs introduced as tradeoffs for its increased power and realism, not the least of which involves complicated problems of estimation and identification. But reading this volume should broaden the reader's view and introduce him or her to the fruitful intersection of psychometrics and econometrics, which has only recently begun to penetrate the practicing social scientist's consciousness.

—*John L. Sullivan*
Series Co-Editor

COVARIANCE STRUCTURE MODELS
An Introduction to LISREL

J. SCOTT LONG
Washington State University

1. INTRODUCTION

Models for the analysis of covariance structures attempt to explain the relationships among a set of observed variables in terms of a generally smaller number of unobserved variables. As the name of this technique implies, the relationships among the observed variables are characterized by the covariances among those variables, contained in the matrix Σ. This matrix is decomposed by a model that assumes that *unobserved* variables are generating the pattern or structure among the *observed* variables. Using a measurement model linking the observed variables to the unobserved variables, and a structural model relating the unobserved variables, an analysis of the covariance matrix Σ is made to describe its structure.

The term "analysis of covariance structures" was introduced by Bock and Bargmann (1966) to describe what would now be called a confirmatory factor model. Since then, numerous authors (including Browne, Bentler, Goldberger, Jöreskog, Lee, Sörbom, McDonald, and Múthen) have added to the complexity and generality of the model. The model has grown from the factor analytic model of Bock and Bargmann to an extremely general model in which the covariance matrix Σ is considered to be any function of any set of parameters, with many intermediate forms of the model appearing along the way. See Bentler and Weeks (1979) for a review of these models, or Bentler (1980) for a less mathematically demanding review.

Though progress has been made in the estimation and application of these extremely general forms of the model, our emphasis is on the more limited, albeit still quite general, form introduced by Jöreskog (1973;

Jöreskog and van Thillo, 1972), Keesling (1972), and Wiley (1973). In this more restrictive model the covariances among the observed variables are decomposed in two conceptually distinct steps. First, the observed variables are linked to unobserved or latent variables through a factor analytic model, similar to that commonly found in psychometrics. Second, the causal relationships among these latent variables are specified through a structural equation model, similar to that found in econometrics. The covariance structure model, in the form considered here, consists of the simultaneous specification of a factor model and a structural equation model, and as such represents a fruitful unification of psychometrics and econometrics. This synthesis was greatly facilitated by Goldberger's (1971) programmatic article and the Conference on Structural Equation Models, organized by Goldberger in 1970 (Goldberger and Duncan, 1973).

The application of the covariance structure model in any form requires the use of efficient numerical methods for the maximization of functions of many variables. A major breakthrough in this area was made by K. Jöreskog in 1966 while working at Educational Testing Service. A series of increasingly general programs were developed leading to the well-known and widely available program LISREL (Jöreskog and van Thillo, 1972; Jöreskog and Sörbom, 1976, 1978, 1981), now in its fifth enhancement. This program has played such a vital role in the acceptance and application of the covariance structure model that such models are often referred to as "LISREL models."

The form of the covariance structure model that is presented here is esentially that incorporated in LISREL and will be referred to simply as the covariance stucture model. The decision to restrict attention to this form of the model is motivated by three considerations. First, a number of programs are available for estimation. This is an important consideration, since without such software the model cannot be applied. Second, the mathematical development of the more general models requires techniques beyond those assumed for this monograph. Third, this form of the model includes a wide variety of useful applications, including confirmatory factor analysis, second-order factor models, multiple indicator models, simultaneous equation systems, panel models, and structural equation models with errors in equations and errors in variables. Thus, it should be sufficient for the needs of most researchers.

Our approach to developing the covariance structure model is to present the factor analytic and structural equation models separately before merging them to create the covariance structure model. In the companion volume—*Confirmatory Factor Analysis* (CFA)—in this series, the confirmatory factor model was developed. In Chapter 2 of this volume the measurement component of the covariance structure model is presented as a pair of confirmatory factor models, each similar to the model in *CFA*. In Chapter 3 the structural equation model is presented as a special case of the covariance structure model, consisting only of the structural component of the model. Chapter 4 presents the covariance structure model as a synthesis of the factor model of Chapter 2 and the structural equation model of Chapter 3.

Before beginning, a general overview of the mathematical structures of each model is useful.

The Mathematical Models

The factor analytic model assumes that the observed variables are generated by a generally smaller number of unobserved or latent variables called factors. Observed variables are considered to be measured with error. Thus, the factor model is basically a measurement model. For example, consider the model in Figure 1.1. The squares correspond to observed variables that are measured with error; the circles correspond to unobserved variables. Each of the circles at the top is linked to two observed variables, indicating that the observed variables are generated by the unobserved variables, called common factors. The circles at the bottom of the figure are each linked to one observed variable. They correspond to that portion of the observed variable that cannot be accounted for by one of the common factors. As such, they are called unique factors or errors in measurement. While the covariances among the observed variables are known, they are assumed to be contaminated by errors in their measurement. To eliminate the effects of measurement error, the model estimates the covariance between the two common factors at the top of the figure.

For the example in Figure 1.1, the relationships between the latent variables and observed variables can be written as

$$x_1 = \lambda_{11}\xi_1 + \delta_1 \qquad x_2 = \lambda_{21}\xi_1 + \delta_2$$

$$x_3 = \lambda_{32}\xi_2 + \delta_3 \qquad x_4 = \lambda_{42}\xi_2 + \delta_4 \qquad [1.1]$$

The x's are the observed variables, the ξ's are the common factors, and the δ's are the unique factors. The λ's are loadings, which indicate how a change in a common factor affects an observed variable.

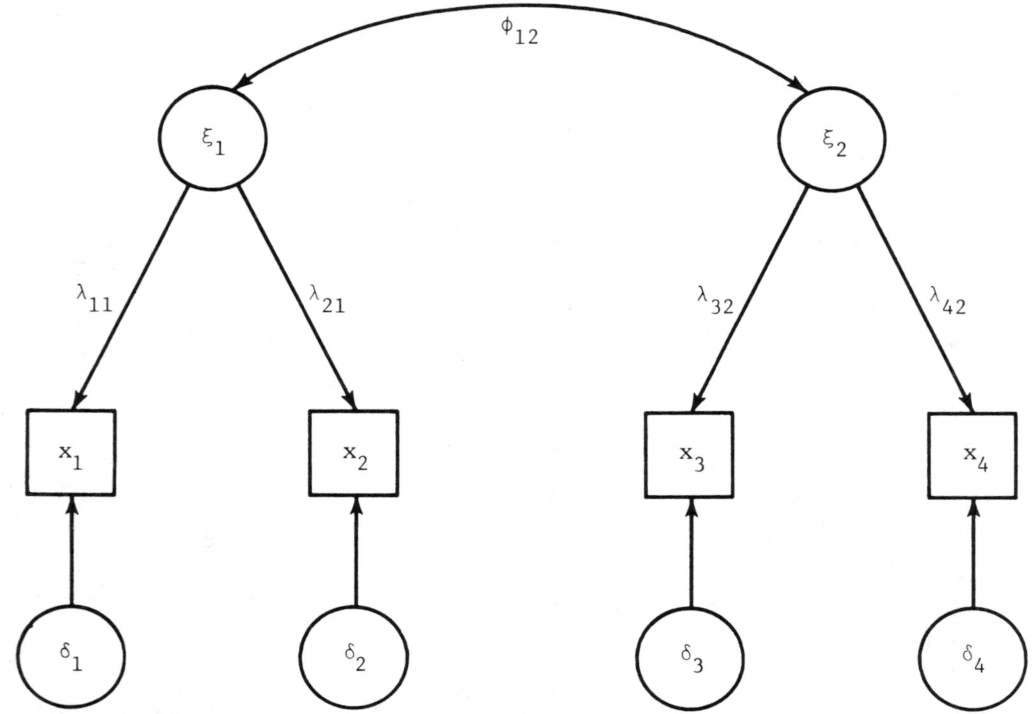

Figure 1.1 The Measurement Component of the Covariance Structure Model

In its general form, the relationships between the observed and latent variables are represented by the matrix equation (equation 2.4 of *CFA*):

$$\mathbf{x} = \mathbf{\Lambda}\boldsymbol{\xi} + \boldsymbol{\delta} \qquad [1.2]$$

where $\mathbf{x}$ is a vector of observed variables, $\boldsymbol{\xi}$ is a vector of common factors, and $\boldsymbol{\delta}$ is a vector of unique factors. Statistically, the task is to explain the interrelationships among the observed variables, as indicated by the covariances among these variables, in terms of relationships among the observed and latent variables defined by equation 1.2. This model was the subject of *CFA*.

The structural equation model has received widespread use in the social and behavioral sciences. In its simplest form it consists of the regression of a single dependent variable on one or more independent variables. An example of such a model, where all variables are assumed to be measured from their means, is

$$y = \beta_1 x_1 + \beta_2 x_2 + e \qquad [1.3]$$

where y is a dependent variable; the x's are independent variables related to the dependent variables by the slope coefficients β_1 and β_2; and e is an *error in equation,* indicating that the x's do not perfectly predict y. In the notation to be used in Chapters 3 and 4, equation 1.3 would be written as

$$\eta_1 = \gamma_{11}\xi_1 + \gamma_{12}\xi_2 + \zeta_1$$

More realistic models are constructed using multiple equation systems, both with and without reciprocal causation. An example of such a model is contained in Figure 1.2. This model states that the observed variable η_1 is causally determined by the observed variables η_2, ξ_1, and ξ_2. That these three variables do not perfectly explain η_1 is reflected by the error in equation ζ_1. Similarly, η_2 is causally determined by η_1, ξ_2, and ξ_3, with an error in equation ζ_2. These structural relations would be written as

$$\eta_1 = \beta_{12}\eta_2 + \gamma_{11}\xi_1 + \gamma_{12}\xi_2 + \zeta_1$$

$$\eta_2 = \beta_{21}\eta_1 + \gamma_{22}\xi_2 + \gamma_{23}\xi_3 + \zeta_2 \qquad [1.4]$$

In its general form the structural equations are written as

$$\boldsymbol{\eta} = \mathbf{B}\boldsymbol{\eta} + \mathbf{\Gamma}\boldsymbol{\xi} + \boldsymbol{\zeta} \qquad [1.5]$$

where $\boldsymbol{\eta}$ is a vector of observed dependent variables measured without error; $\boldsymbol{\xi}$ is a vector of observed independent variables measured without error; $\boldsymbol{\zeta}$ is a vector of errors in equations; **B** is a matrix of coefficients relating the dependent variables to one another; and $\boldsymbol{\Gamma}$ is a matrix of coefficients relating the independent variables to the dependent variables. Special cases of equation 1.5 include multiple regression, path analysis, simultaneous equation systems, and panel analysis. This model is developed in Chapter 3.

The factor analytic and structural equation models are complementary. In the structural equation model the assumption that the variables are measured without error is often unrealistic, requiring the introduction of errors in variables or measurement error. Those using the factor model, in which errors in variables are of major concern, are often interested in making statements about the structural relationships among the unobserved factors. That is, there is a need for a structural equation model relating the factors. The result of the converging needs of those using structural equation models and factor models is the covariance structure model. The covariance structure model allows both errors in variables, as in the factor analytic model, and errors in equations, as in the structural equation model.

Figure 1.3 presents a simple example of the covariance structure model. The structural relationships in Figure 1.3 are identical to those in Figure 1.2, used to illustrate the structural equation model. The difference is that the structural relations in the covariance structure model are among latent variables, rather than observed variables. In the covariance structure model, latent variables are linked to observed variables in the same way as in the factor model. This is represented in Figure 1.3 by the lines linking the x's and y's in squares to the η's and ξ's in circles. The equations specifying these links are similar to those in Equation 1.1. For the dependent variables, the measurement model is

$$y_1 = \lambda^y_{11}\eta_1 + \epsilon_1 \qquad y_2 = \lambda^y_{21}\eta_1 + \epsilon_2$$

$$y_3 = \lambda^y_{32}\eta_2 + \epsilon_3 \qquad y_4 = \lambda^y_{42}\eta_2 + \epsilon_4$$

For the independent variables, the measurement model is

$$x_1 = \lambda^x_{11}\xi_1 + \delta_1 \qquad x_2 = \lambda^x_{21}\xi_1 + \delta_2 \qquad x_3 = \lambda^x_{32}\xi_2 + \delta_3$$

$$x_4 = \lambda^x_{42}\xi_2 + \delta_4 \qquad x_5 = \lambda^x_{53}\xi_3 + \delta_5 \qquad x_6 = \lambda^x_{63}\xi_3 + \delta_6$$

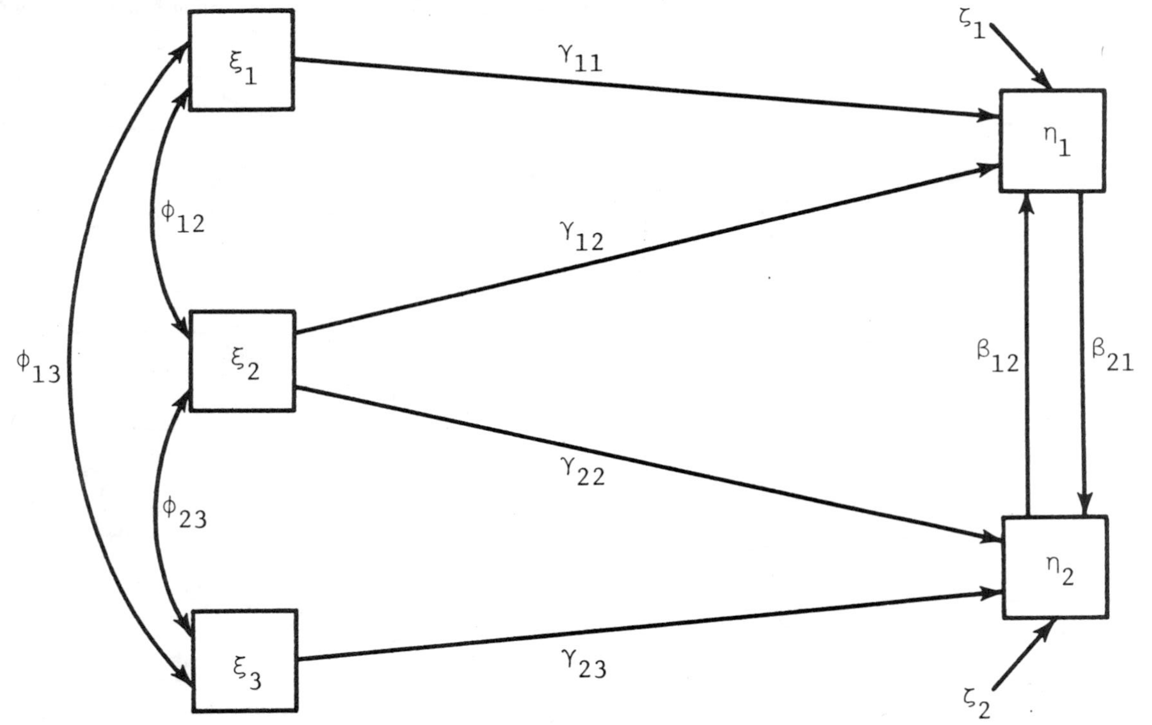

Figure 1.2 The Structural Component of the Covariance Structure Model

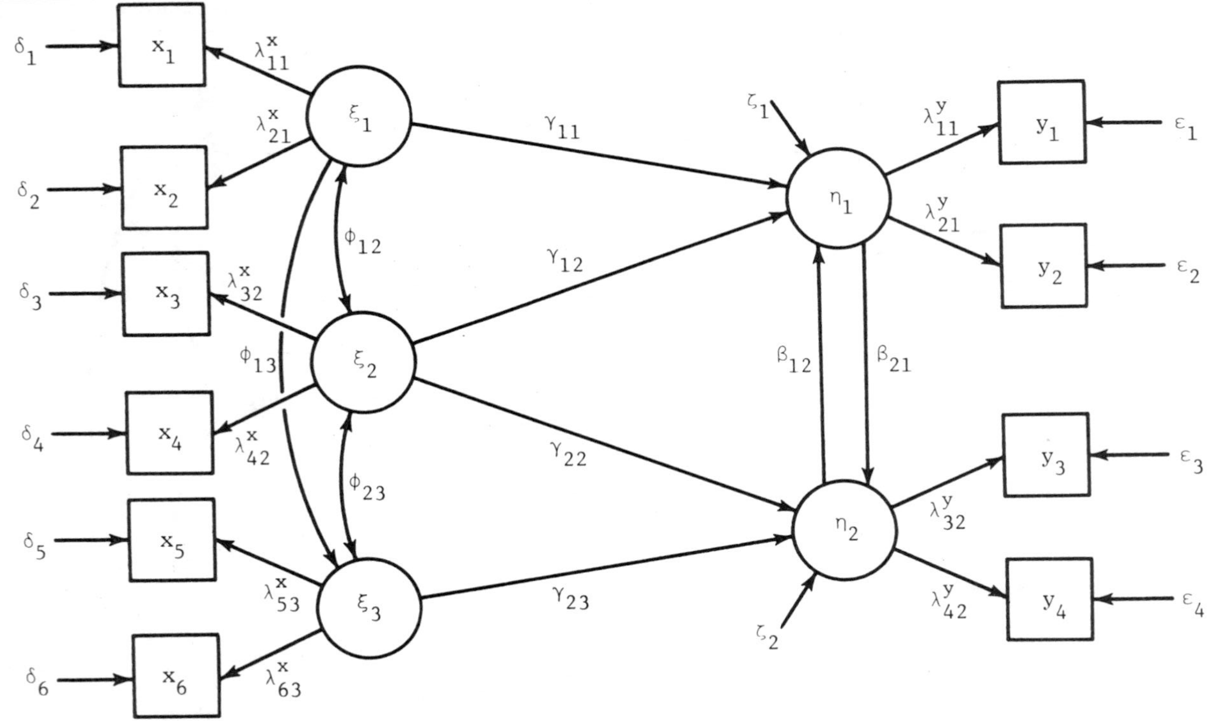

Figure 1.3 Combined Measurement Component and Structural Component of the Covariance Structure Model

In its general form, the covariance structure model consists of three equations. First, a structural equation model specifies the causal relationships among latent variables:

$$\boldsymbol{\eta} = \mathbf{B}\boldsymbol{\eta} + \boldsymbol{\Gamma}\boldsymbol{\xi} + \boldsymbol{\zeta} \qquad [1.6]$$

This equation has the same form as equation 1.5, the only difference being that $\boldsymbol{\eta}$ and $\boldsymbol{\xi}$ now contain latent variables rather than observed variables.

The second and third equations are a pair of measurement models formally similar to equation 1.2. In the first measurement model the observed x-variables are linked by the loading matrix $\boldsymbol{\Lambda}_x$ to the latent ξ-variables:

$$\mathbf{x} = \boldsymbol{\Lambda}_x\boldsymbol{\xi} + \boldsymbol{\delta} \qquad [1.7]$$

Errors in the measurement of $\mathbf{x}$ are contained in $\boldsymbol{\delta}$. In the second measurement model the observed y-variables are linked by the loading matrix $\boldsymbol{\Lambda}_y$ to the latent η-variables:

$$\mathbf{y} = \boldsymbol{\Lambda}_y\boldsymbol{\eta} + \boldsymbol{\epsilon} \qquad [1.8]$$

Errors in the measurement of $\mathbf{y}$ are contained in $\boldsymbol{\epsilon}$. The measurement equations 1.7 and 1.8, along with the structural equation 1.6, make up the covariance structure model that is developed in Chapter 4.

2. THE MEASUREMENT MODEL

The measurement component of the covariance structure model consists of a pair of confirmatory factor models formally identical to those developed in *CFA*. This chapter provides a formal specification of the two factor models and the assumptions linking them. The parameters of these models can be identified, estimated, tested, and interpreted in exactly the same way as the parameters of the single factor model presented in *CFA;* accordingly, these issues are not addressed here.

Specification of the Measurement Model

The covariance structure model has two sets of common factors. $\boldsymbol{\xi}$ contains s common factors that are related to q observed variables contained in $\mathbf{x}$. $\boldsymbol{\eta}$ contains r common factors that are related to p observed variables contained in $\mathbf{y}$. In the structural component of the covariance structure model the ξ's are unobserved exogenous variables, and the η's are unobserved endogenous variables. (These terms are defined in Chapter 3.) The observed variables and common factors are linked by a pair of factor equations:

$$\mathbf{x} = \boldsymbol{\Lambda}_x \boldsymbol{\xi} + \boldsymbol{\delta} \qquad [2.1]$$

$$\mathbf{y} = \boldsymbol{\Lambda}_y \boldsymbol{\eta} + \boldsymbol{\epsilon} \qquad [2.2]$$

$\boldsymbol{\Lambda}_x$ is a $(q \times s)$ matrix of the loadings of the x's on the ξ's, with the loading of x_i on ξ_j being designated as λ^x_{ij}. $\boldsymbol{\delta}$ is a $(q \times 1)$ vector of unique factors or errors in measurement that affect the x's. Similarly, $\boldsymbol{\Lambda}_y$ is a $(p \times r)$ matrix of loadings of the y's on the η's, with the loading of y_i on η_j being designated as λ^y_{ij}. And, $\boldsymbol{\epsilon}$ is a $(p \times 1)$ vector of unique factors that affect the y's. Each of the variables is assumed to be measured as a deviation from its mean:

$$E(\mathbf{x}) = E(\boldsymbol{\delta}) = \mathbf{0} \qquad E(\boldsymbol{\xi}) = \mathbf{0}$$

$$E(\mathbf{y}) = E(\boldsymbol{\epsilon}) = \mathbf{0} \qquad E(\boldsymbol{\eta}) = \mathbf{0}$$

Within each equation, the common factors and unique factors are assumed to be uncorrelated. Specifically it is assumed that

$$E(\boldsymbol{\xi}\boldsymbol{\delta}') = \mathbf{0} \quad \text{or} \quad E(\boldsymbol{\delta}\boldsymbol{\xi}') = \mathbf{0}$$

$$E(\boldsymbol{\eta}\boldsymbol{\epsilon}') = \mathbf{0} \quad \text{or} \quad E(\boldsymbol{\epsilon}\boldsymbol{\eta}') = \mathbf{0}$$

These and other assumptions are summarized in Table 2.1.

The variances and covariances of the ξ's are contained in the $(s \times s)$ covariance matrix $\boldsymbol{\Phi}$. The covariance matrix for the δ's is the $(q \times q)$, symmetric, and not necessarily diagonal, matrix $\boldsymbol{\Theta}_\delta$. The covariance matrix for the ϵ's is a similar $(p \times p)$ matrix $\boldsymbol{\Theta}_\epsilon$. The variances and covariances of the η's are contained in the $(r \times r)$ symmetric matrix $COV(\boldsymbol{\eta})$. This matrix is not given a unique letter (such as $\boldsymbol{\Phi}$ for the ξ's) since in the full covariance structure model it will be defined in terms of other parameters of the model. How this is done is described in Chapter 3 and need not concern us here.

Specification of the measurement portion of the covariance structure model involves imposing substantively motivated constraints on the

TABLE 2.1
Summary of the Measurement Component of the Covariance Structure Model

Matrix	*Dimension*	*Mean*	*Covariance*	*Dimension*	*Description*
$\boldsymbol{\xi}$	$(s \times 1)$	$\mathbf{0}$	$\boldsymbol{\Phi} = E(\boldsymbol{\xi\xi}')$	$(s \times s)$	common exogenous factors
$\mathbf{x}$	$(q \times 1)$	$\mathbf{0}$	$\boldsymbol{\Sigma}_{xx} = E(\mathbf{xx}')$	$(q \times q)$	observed exogenous variables
$\boldsymbol{\Lambda}_x$	$(q \times s)$	—	—	—	loadings of $\mathbf{x}$ on $\boldsymbol{\xi}$
$\boldsymbol{\delta}$	$(q \times 1)$	$\mathbf{0}$	$\boldsymbol{\Theta}_\delta = E(\boldsymbol{\delta\delta}')$	$(q \times q)$	unique factors for $\mathbf{x}$
$\boldsymbol{\eta}$	$(r \times 1)$	$\mathbf{0}$	$COV(\boldsymbol{\eta}) = E(\boldsymbol{\eta\eta}')$	$(r \times r)$	common endogenous factors
$\mathbf{y}$	$(p \times 1)$	$\mathbf{0}$	$\boldsymbol{\Sigma}_{yy} = E(\mathbf{yy}')$	$(p \times p)$	observed endogenous variables
$\boldsymbol{\Lambda}_y$	$(p \times r)$	—	—	—	loadings of $\mathbf{y}$ on $\boldsymbol{\eta}$
$\boldsymbol{\epsilon}$	$(p \times 1)$	$\mathbf{0}$	$\boldsymbol{\Theta}_\epsilon = E(\boldsymbol{\epsilon\epsilon}')$	$(p \times p)$	unique factors for $\mathbf{y}$

Factor Equations:

$$\mathbf{x} = \boldsymbol{\Lambda}_x\boldsymbol{\xi} + \boldsymbol{\delta} \qquad [2.1]$$

$$\mathbf{y} = \boldsymbol{\Lambda}_y\boldsymbol{\eta} + \boldsymbol{\epsilon} \qquad [2.2]$$

Covariance Equation

$$\boldsymbol{\Sigma} = \left[\begin{array}{c|c} \boldsymbol{\Lambda}_y COV(\boldsymbol{\eta})\boldsymbol{\Lambda}_y' + \boldsymbol{\Theta}_\epsilon & \boldsymbol{\Lambda}_y COV(\boldsymbol{\eta},\boldsymbol{\xi})\boldsymbol{\Lambda}_x' \\ \hline \boldsymbol{\Lambda}_x COV(\boldsymbol{\xi},\boldsymbol{\eta})\boldsymbol{\Lambda}_y' & \boldsymbol{\Lambda}_x\boldsymbol{\Phi}\boldsymbol{\Lambda}_x' + \boldsymbol{\Theta}_\delta \end{array}\right] \qquad [2.3]$$

Assumptions:

a. Variables are measured from their means: $E(\mathbf{x}) = E(\boldsymbol{\delta}) = \mathbf{0}$; $E(\boldsymbol{\xi}) = \mathbf{0}$; $E(\mathbf{y}) = E(\boldsymbol{\epsilon}) = \mathbf{0}$; $E(\boldsymbol{\eta}) = \mathbf{0}$.

b. Common and unique factors are uncorrelated: $E(\boldsymbol{\xi\delta}') = \mathbf{0}$ or $E(\boldsymbol{\delta\xi}') = \mathbf{0}$; $E(\boldsymbol{\eta\epsilon}') = \mathbf{0}$ or $E(\boldsymbol{\epsilon\eta}') = \mathbf{0}$; $E(\boldsymbol{\xi\epsilon}') = \mathbf{0}$ or $E(\boldsymbol{\epsilon\xi}') = \mathbf{0}$; $E(\boldsymbol{\eta\delta}') = \mathbf{0}$ or $E(\boldsymbol{\delta\eta}') = \mathbf{0}$.

c. Unique factors are uncorrelated across equations: $E(\boldsymbol{\delta\epsilon}') = \mathbf{0}$ or $E(\boldsymbol{\epsilon\delta}') = \mathbf{0}$.

parameter matrices: $\boldsymbol{\Lambda}_x$, $\boldsymbol{\Lambda}_y$, $\boldsymbol{\Phi}$, $\boldsymbol{\Theta}_\delta$, and $\boldsymbol{\Theta}_\epsilon$. These constraints can be either restrictions on parameters to equal fixed values and/or restrictions on sets of parameters to be equal.

At this point each of the factor models in equations 2.1 and 2.2 appears to be identical to the model described in *CFA*. Equation 2.1 is identical to the model in *CFA* if $\boldsymbol{\Lambda}_x$ is replaced by $\boldsymbol{\Lambda}$; and equation 2.2 is identical if $\mathbf{y}$, $\boldsymbol{\Lambda}_y$, $\boldsymbol{\eta}$, $COV(\boldsymbol{\eta})$, and $\boldsymbol{\epsilon}$ are replaced by $\mathbf{x}$, $\boldsymbol{\Lambda}$, $\boldsymbol{\xi}$, $\boldsymbol{\Phi}$, and $\boldsymbol{\delta}$. New assumptions are necessary, however, when the links between the two models are considered.

Relationships Between the Two Factor Models

While some of the variables are correlated across the two factor models, others are assumed to be uncorrelated. The observed x's and y's can be correlated. Their covariances are contained in the $(q \times p)$ matrix Σ_{xy}, whose $(i,j)^{th}$ element is the covariance between x_i and y_j. Similarly, the exogenous ξ-factors and endogenous η-factors can be correlated. Their covariances are contained in the $(s \times r)$ matrix $COV(\boldsymbol{\xi},\boldsymbol{\eta})$, or the $(r \times s)$ matrix $COV(\boldsymbol{\eta}, \boldsymbol{\xi})$.

Just as the unique factors are assumed to be uncorrelated with the common factors in their own factor equation, they are assumed to be uncorrelated with the common factors in the other equation. Thus, it is assumed that

$$E(\boldsymbol{\xi}\boldsymbol{\epsilon}') = \mathbf{0} \quad \text{or} \quad E(\boldsymbol{\epsilon}\boldsymbol{\xi}') = \mathbf{0}$$

$$E(\boldsymbol{\eta}\boldsymbol{\delta}') = \mathbf{0} \quad \text{or} \quad E(\boldsymbol{\delta}\boldsymbol{\eta}') = \mathbf{0}$$

While the δ's can be correlated among themselves, and the ϵ's can be correlated among themselves, it is assumed that the δ's and ϵ's are uncorrelated. That is,

$$E(\boldsymbol{\delta}\boldsymbol{\epsilon}') = \mathbf{0} \quad \text{or} \quad E(\boldsymbol{\epsilon}\boldsymbol{\delta}') = \mathbf{0}$$

Finally, it is assumed that the observed x's do not load on the latent η's, and that the observed y's do not load on the latent ξ's.

These ideas are illustrated in Figure 2.1. The circles represent latent variables, and the squares represent observed variables. Curved arrows linking two variables indicate that those variables are correlated; straight arrows indicate that the variable pointing affects the variable being pointed at. A heavy solid line separates portions of the model across which loadings or correlations cannot occur.

The Covariance Structure

Since the ξ's and η's are not observed, the parameters of the model must be estimated by means of the links between the variances and covariances of the observed variables and the parameters of the model. While estimation of the confirmatory factor model is not of concern to

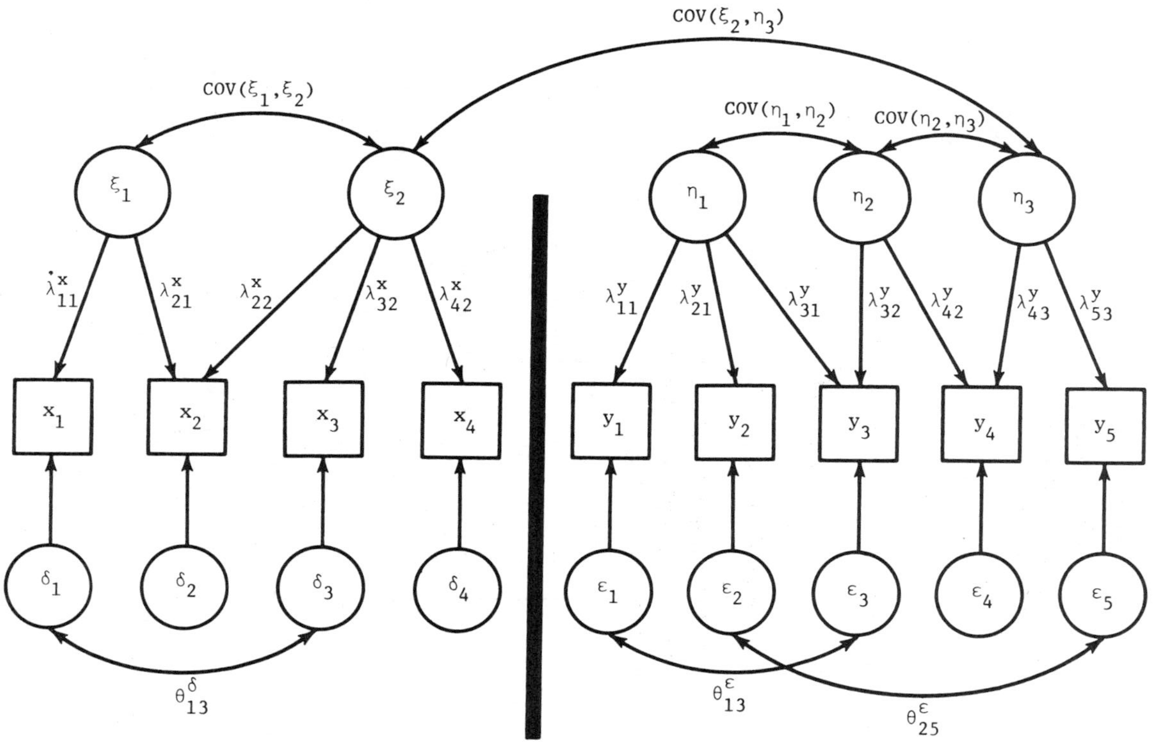

Figure 2.1 The Measurement Component of the Covariance Structure Model

us here (it has been fully considered in *CFA*), it is useful to consider the links between the observed variances and covariances and the parameters.

Let $\boldsymbol{\Sigma}$ be the population matrix of variances and covariances of the observed variables. This matrix is defined as

$$\boldsymbol{\Sigma} = \mathrm{E}\left[\begin{bmatrix}\mathbf{y}\\ \hline \mathbf{x}\end{bmatrix}\begin{bmatrix}\mathbf{y}\\ \hline \mathbf{x}\end{bmatrix}'\right] = \left[\begin{array}{c|c}\mathrm{E}(\mathbf{yy}') & \mathrm{E}(\mathbf{yx}')\\ \hline \mathrm{E}(\mathbf{xy}') & \mathrm{E}(\mathbf{xx}')\end{array}\right]$$

Substituting the values for **x** and **y** contained in equations 2.1 and 2.2

$$\boldsymbol{\Sigma} = \left[\begin{array}{c|c}\mathrm{E}[(\boldsymbol{\Lambda}_y\boldsymbol{\eta} + \boldsymbol{\epsilon})(\boldsymbol{\Lambda}_y\boldsymbol{\eta} + \boldsymbol{\epsilon})'] & \mathrm{E}[(\boldsymbol{\Lambda}_y\boldsymbol{\eta} + \boldsymbol{\epsilon})(\boldsymbol{\Lambda}_x\boldsymbol{\xi} + \boldsymbol{\delta})']\\ \hline \mathrm{E}[(\boldsymbol{\Lambda}_x\boldsymbol{\xi} + \boldsymbol{\delta})(\boldsymbol{\Lambda}_y\boldsymbol{\eta} + \boldsymbol{\epsilon})'] & \mathrm{E}[(\boldsymbol{\Lambda}_x\boldsymbol{\xi} + \boldsymbol{\delta})(\boldsymbol{\Lambda}_x\boldsymbol{\xi} + \boldsymbol{\delta})']\end{array}\right]$$

After taking the transposes, making the necessary multiplications, taking expectations, and applying the assumptions about certain vectors of variables being uncorrelated, $\boldsymbol{\Sigma}$ can be written as

$$\boldsymbol{\Sigma} = \left[\begin{array}{c|c}\boldsymbol{\Lambda}_y\mathrm{COV}(\boldsymbol{\eta})\boldsymbol{\Lambda}_y' + \boldsymbol{\Theta}_\epsilon & \boldsymbol{\Lambda}_y\mathrm{COV}(\boldsymbol{\eta},\boldsymbol{\xi})\boldsymbol{\Lambda}_x'\\ \hline \boldsymbol{\Lambda}_x\mathrm{COV}(\boldsymbol{\xi},\boldsymbol{\eta})\,\boldsymbol{\Lambda}_y' & \boldsymbol{\Lambda}_x\boldsymbol{\Phi}\boldsymbol{\Lambda}_x' + \boldsymbol{\Theta}_\delta\end{array}\right] \qquad [2.3]$$

The reader may want to work out the derivation of equation 2.3, although it is not essential for understanding the model. What is important to realize is that equation 2.3 decomposes the variances and covariances of the observed x's and y's into a function of the loading matrices Λ_x and Λ_y, the variances and covariances of the ξ's and η's, and the variances and covariances of the δ's and ϵ's. Constraints imposed on the parameter matrices structure the covariance matrix $\boldsymbol{\Sigma}$. Estimation proceeds by finding estimates of the parameters that reproduce the sample variances and covariances of the observed variables according to equation 2.3 as closely as possible. Thus, equation 2.3 serves the same purpose as the covariance equation derived for the single confirmatory factor model in *CFA*.

Summary

This concludes our description of the measurement component of the covariance structure model. While the confirmatory factor model was developed in *CFA* as a powerful model in its own right, here it is used to relate observed variables to factors, with the intention of specifying a set of structural relations among these factors. How structural relations are specified is considered in the next chapter.

3. THE STRUCTURAL EQUATION MODEL

The second component of the covariance structure model is a structural equation model causally relating the latent variables that have been factored from observed variables through a measurement model. This chapter simplifies the covariance structure model by assuming that the latent variables are observed. This simplification facilitates understanding of the structural component of the covariance structure model and allows us to take advantage of the vast econometric literature on structural equation models for observed variables (in order of increasing difficulty, see Hanushek and Jackson, 1977; Wonnacott and Wonnacott, 1979; Theil, 1971). The issues of specification, identification, and interpretation developed in this chapter for observed variables are directly applicable to the structural equation model for latent variables in Chapter 4.

A second advantage of presenting the structural component without considering measurement error is that software developed for the covariance structure model is extremely useful for estimating structural equation models that incorporate equality constraints on structural parameters and/or the specification of zero covariances among some but not all of the errors in equations. Such constraints are increasingly common in social science applications, and particularly in panel models. Indeed, the most thorough treatment of panel models to date (Kessler and Greenberg, 1981) suggests that panel models be estimated with software for the covariance structure model, but it does not indicate how this is to be done. A secondary purpose of this chapter is to fill this gap in the literature on panel models.

The Mathematical Model

A structural equation model specifies the causal relationships among a set of variables. Those variables that are to be explained by the model are called *endogenous* variables. Endogenous variables are explained by specifying that they are causally dependent on other endogenous variables and/or what are called *exogenous* variables. Exogenous variables are determined outside of the model and, accordingly, are not explained by the model.

Let $\boldsymbol{\eta}$ be a (r × 1) vector of endogenous variables, and let $\boldsymbol{\xi}$ be a (s × 1) vector of exogenous variables. The model assumes that the variables are related by a system of linear structural equations.

$$\boldsymbol{\eta} = \mathbf{B}\boldsymbol{\eta} + \boldsymbol{\Gamma}\boldsymbol{\xi} + \boldsymbol{\zeta} \qquad [3.1]$$

where $\mathbf{B}$ is a (r × r) matrix of coefficients relating the endogenous variables to one another; and $\boldsymbol{\Gamma}$ is a (r × s) matrix of coefficients relating the exogenous variables to the endogenous variables. $\boldsymbol{\zeta}$ is a (r × 1) vector of errors in equations, indicating that the endogenous variables are not perfectly predicted by the structural equations.

Equation 3.1 is thought of as a *structural* equation, since it describes the assumed causal structure of the process being modeled. Restricting elements of $\mathbf{B}$ and $\boldsymbol{\Gamma}$ to equal zero indicates the absence of a causal relationship between the appropriate variables. Fixing the $(i,j)^{th}$ element of $\boldsymbol{\Gamma}$ to zero ($\gamma_{ij} = 0$) implies that the exogenous variable ξ_j does not have a causal effect on the endogenous variable η_i. Similarly, if the $(i,j)^{th}$ element of $\mathbf{B}$ is fixed to be zero ($\beta_{ij} = 0$), the endogenous variable η_i is assumed to be unaffected by η_j. The diagonal elements of $\mathbf{B}$ are assumed to equal zero, indicating that an endogenous variable does not cause itself.

Equation 3.1 can be rewritten by adding $-\mathbf{B}\boldsymbol{\eta}$ to each side, resulting in $\boldsymbol{\eta} - \mathbf{B}\boldsymbol{\eta} = \boldsymbol{\Gamma}\boldsymbol{\xi} + \boldsymbol{\zeta}$, or defining $\ddot{\mathbf{B}}$ as $(\mathbf{I} - \mathbf{B})$:

$$\ddot{\mathbf{B}}\boldsymbol{\eta} = \boldsymbol{\Gamma}\boldsymbol{\xi} + \boldsymbol{\zeta} \qquad [3.2]$$

While this form of the structural equation model is more common in the econometric literature, the form presented in equation 3.1 is slightly more convenient to interpret. A positive value in $\mathbf{B}$ indicates a positive relationship between two endogenous variables, whereas a positive value in $\ddot{\mathbf{B}}$ indicates a negative relationship. Since $\ddot{\mathbf{B}}$ is more convenient for stating a number of results, it is used as a shorthand notation for $(\mathbf{I} - \mathbf{B})$.

All variables are assumed to be measured as deviations from their means: $E(\boldsymbol{\eta}) = E(\boldsymbol{\zeta}) = \mathbf{0}$ and $E(\boldsymbol{\xi}) = \mathbf{0}$. This does not affect the generality of the model, since the structural parameters contained in $\mathbf{B}$ and $\boldsymbol{\Gamma}$ are not affected by this assumption.

Just as common factors and unique factors are assumed to be uncorrelated in the factor model, the errors in equations and the exogenous variables are assumed to be uncorrelated in the structural equation model. That is, $E(\boldsymbol{\xi}\boldsymbol{\zeta}') = \mathbf{0}$, or equivalently, that $E(\boldsymbol{\zeta}\boldsymbol{\xi}') = \mathbf{0}$.

TABLE 3.1
Summary of the Structural Component of the Covariance Structure Model

Matrix	*Dimension*	*Mean*	*Covariance*	*Dimension*	*Description*
$\boldsymbol{\eta}$	$(r \times 1)$	**0**	$COV(\boldsymbol{\eta}) = E(\boldsymbol{\eta\eta}')$	$(r \times r)$	endogenous variables
$\boldsymbol{\xi}$	$(s \times 1)$	**0**	$\boldsymbol{\Phi} = E(\boldsymbol{\xi\xi}')$	$(s \times s)$	exogenous variables
$\boldsymbol{\zeta}$	$(r \times 1)$	**0**	$\boldsymbol{\Psi} = E(\boldsymbol{\zeta\zeta}')$	$(r \times r)$	errors in equations
$\mathbf{B}$	$(r \times r)$	—	—	—	direct effects of $\boldsymbol{\eta}$ on $\boldsymbol{\eta}$
$\ddot{\mathbf{B}}$	$(r \times r)$	—	—	—	defined as $(\mathbf{I} - \mathbf{B})$
$\boldsymbol{\Gamma}$	$(r \times s)$	—	—	—	direct effects of $\boldsymbol{\xi}$ on $\boldsymbol{\eta}$

Structural Equations:

$$\boldsymbol{\eta} = \mathbf{B}\boldsymbol{\eta} + \boldsymbol{\Gamma\xi} + \boldsymbol{\zeta} \qquad [3.1]$$

$$\ddot{\mathbf{B}}\boldsymbol{\eta} = \boldsymbol{\Gamma\xi} + \boldsymbol{\zeta} \qquad [3.2]$$

Reduced Form Equation:

$$\boldsymbol{\eta} = \ddot{\mathbf{B}}^{-1}\boldsymbol{\Gamma\xi} + \ddot{\mathbf{B}}^{-1}\boldsymbol{\zeta} \qquad [3.4]$$

Covariance Equation:

$$\boldsymbol{\Sigma} = \left[\begin{array}{c|c} \ddot{\mathbf{B}}^{-1}(\boldsymbol{\Gamma\Phi\Gamma}' + \boldsymbol{\Psi})\ddot{\mathbf{B}}'^{-1} & \ddot{\mathbf{B}}^{-1}\boldsymbol{\Gamma\Phi} \\ \hline \boldsymbol{\Phi\Gamma}'\ddot{\mathbf{B}}'^{-1} & \boldsymbol{\Phi} \end{array}\right] \qquad [3.5]$$

Assumptions:

a. Variables are measured from their means: $E(\boldsymbol{\eta}) = E(\boldsymbol{\zeta}) = \mathbf{0}$; $E(\boldsymbol{\xi}) = \mathbf{0}$.

b. Exogenous variables and errors in equations are uncorrelated: $E(\boldsymbol{\xi\zeta}') = \mathbf{0}$ or $E(\boldsymbol{\zeta\xi}') = \mathbf{0}$.

c. None of the structural equations is redundant: $\ddot{\mathbf{B}}^{-1} = (\mathbf{I} - \mathbf{B})^{-1}$ exists.

It is also assumed that $\ddot{\mathbf{B}} = (\mathbf{I} - \mathbf{B})$ is nonsingular (i.e., that $\ddot{\mathbf{B}}^{-1}$ exists). This assumption is not very restrictive, simply meaning that none of the equations in the model is redundant.

With these assumptions, summarized in Table 3.1, a number of covariance matrices can be defined. The covariance among the errors in equations, the ζ_i's, are contained in the symmetric matrix $\boldsymbol{\Psi}$ of dimension $(r \times r)$. Since the ζ_i's are assumed measured from zero (i.e., $E(\zeta_i) = 0$), $\boldsymbol{\Psi}$ can be defined as: $\boldsymbol{\Psi} = E(\boldsymbol{\zeta\zeta}')$. Values of $\boldsymbol{\Psi}$ are generally unknown, although off-diagonal elements can be restricted to zero to indicate that errors in equations are uncorrelated across two equations. The covariance matrix for the exogenous variables is defined as $\mathbf{\Phi}$, a (s × s) symmetric matrix. Since the exogenous variables are measured from their means, $\mathbf{\Phi} = E(\xi\xi')$.

These ideas and the flexibility of the structural equation model can be illustrated by a series of examples.

Example 3.1: multiple regression. With one endogenous variable (r = 1) and three exogenous variables (s = 3), equation 3.1 is

$$[\eta_1] = [\underline{0}]\,[\eta_1] + [\gamma_{11}\ \gamma_{12}\ \gamma_{13}]\begin{bmatrix}\xi_1\\ \xi_2\\ \xi_3\end{bmatrix} + [\zeta_1]$$

or as it is more commonly written, $\eta_1 = \gamma_{11}\xi_1 + \gamma_{12}\xi_2 + \gamma_{13}\xi_3 + \zeta_1$. (Here and elsewhere, elements of parameter matrices are underlined if they have been constrained to equal the underlined value.) $\mathbf{\Phi}$ contains the population variances and covariances for ξ_1, ξ_2, and ξ_3:

$$\mathbf{\Phi} = \begin{bmatrix} \mathrm{VAR}(\xi_1) & \mathrm{COV}(\xi_1,\xi_2) & \mathrm{COV}(\xi_1,\xi_3) \\ \mathrm{COV}(\xi_2,\xi_1) & \mathrm{VAR}(\xi_2) & \mathrm{COV}(\xi_2,\xi_3) \\ \mathrm{COV}(\xi_3,\xi_1) & \mathrm{COV}(\xi_3,\xi_2) & \mathrm{VAR}(\xi_3) \end{bmatrix} = \begin{bmatrix} \phi_{11} & \phi_{12} & \phi_{13} \\ \phi_{21} & \phi_{22} & \phi_{23} \\ \phi_{31} & \phi_{32} & \phi_{33} \end{bmatrix}$$

$\mathbf{\Psi}$ contains the variance of the only error in equation: $\mathbf{\Psi} = [\psi_{11}]$. This is the simplest structural equation model, and it is equivalent to a single equation, multiple regression model. //[1]

Example 3.2: a panel model. The complexity of Example 3.1 can be increased by considering a system of equations. This example, taken from Wheaton (1978), is a panel analysis of the sociogenesis of psychological disorder. The proposed model, presented in Figure 3.1, specifies the causal relationships among father's socioeconomic status (ξ_1), the respondent's socioeconomic status at three points in time (η_1, η_2, and η_4), and the number of symptoms of psychological disorder at two points in time (η_3 and η_5). In the original article there were two indicators of psychological disorder; in this example a single indicator, which is assumed to be measured without error, is used. The full model with both indicators is presented in Chapter 4.

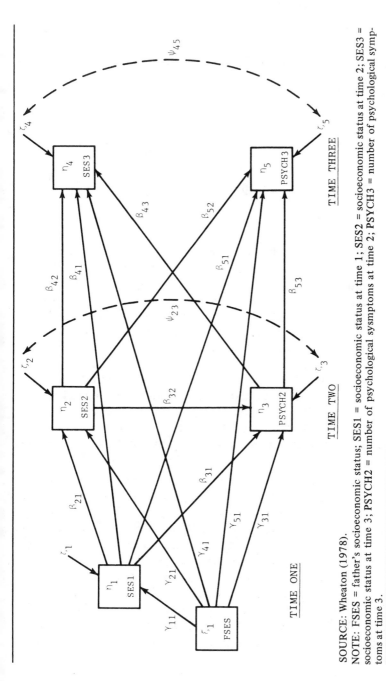

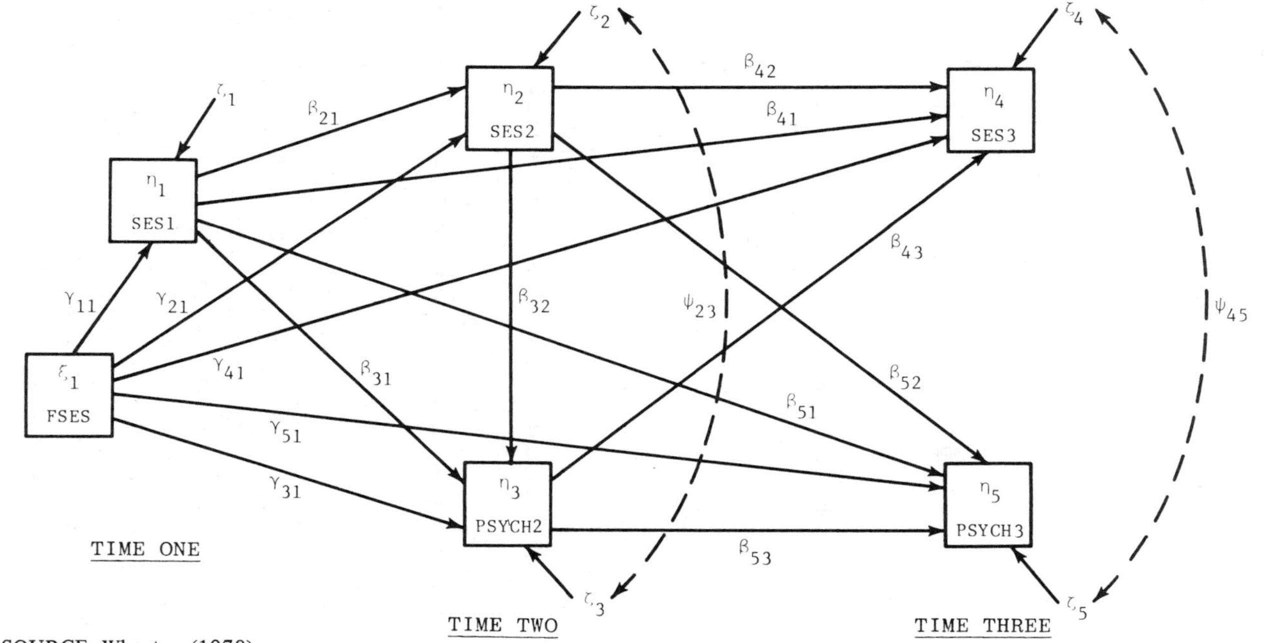

SOURCE: Wheaton (1978).

NOTE: FSES = father's socioeconomic status; SES1 = socioeconomic status at time 1; SES2 = socioeconomic status at time 2; SES3 = socioeconomic status at time 3; PSYCH2 = number of psychological sysmptoms at time 2; PSYCH3 = number of psychological symptoms at time 3.

Figure 3.1 Structural Equation Model for the Sociogenesis of Psychological Disorder

The structural equations for this model can be written as

$$\begin{bmatrix}\eta_1\\ \eta_2\\ \eta_3\\ \eta_4\\ \eta_5\end{bmatrix} = \begin{bmatrix}\underline{0} & \underline{0} & \underline{0} & \underline{0} & \underline{0}\\ \beta_{21} & \underline{0} & \underline{0} & \underline{0} & \underline{0}\\ \beta_{31} & \beta_{32} & \underline{0} & \underline{0} & \underline{0}\\ \beta_{41} & \beta_{42} & \beta_{43} & \underline{0} & \underline{0}\\ \beta_{51} & \beta_{52} & \beta_{53} & \underline{0} & \underline{0}\end{bmatrix} \begin{bmatrix}\eta_1\\ \eta_2\\ \eta_3\\ \eta_4\\ \eta_5\end{bmatrix} + \begin{bmatrix}\gamma_{11}\\ \gamma_{21}\\ \gamma_{31}\\ \gamma_{41}\\ \gamma_{51}\end{bmatrix} \begin{bmatrix}\xi_1\end{bmatrix} + \begin{bmatrix}\zeta_1\\ \zeta_2\\ \zeta_3\\ \zeta_4\\ \zeta_5\end{bmatrix} \qquad [3.3]$$

Since there is only a single exogenous variable, $\mathbf{\Phi} = [\mathrm{VAR}(\xi_1)]$.

The covariances among the errors in equations are contained in $\mathbf{\Psi}$. Two specifications of $\mathbf{\Psi}$ can be considered. In the first specification all errors in equations are assumed to be uncorrelated. That is, $\mathbf{\Psi}$ is restricted to be diagonal. A second, more realistic specification allows some of the errors in equations to be correlated. These correlated errors are indicated by the curved, dashed arrows connecting ζ_2 and ζ_3, and ζ_4 and ζ_5 in Figure 3.1. These covariances indicate that the errors in the equations predicting socioeconomic status (SES) and number of symptoms of psychological disorders at the same period of time are correlated. This might occur if the model were misspecified by the exclusion of variables that affect both SES and number of symptoms. The error caused by this misspecification would be picked up by ζ_2 and ζ_3 at time 2, and ζ_4 and ζ_5 at time 3; accordingly, these pairs of errors would be correlated. These constraints would be incorporated into $\mathbf{\Psi}$ as follows:

$$\mathbf{\Psi} = \begin{bmatrix}\psi_{11} & \underline{0} & \underline{0} & \underline{0} & \underline{0}\\ \underline{0} & \psi_{22} & \psi_{23} & \underline{0} & \underline{0}\\ \underline{0} & \psi_{32} & \psi_{33} & \underline{0} & \underline{0}\\ \underline{0} & \underline{0} & \underline{0} & \psi_{44} & \psi_{45}\\ \underline{0} & \underline{0} & \underline{0} & \psi_{54} & \psi_{55}\end{bmatrix}$$

The importance of the decision on how to specify $\mathbf{\Psi}$ is illustrated in later sections on identification and estimation. //

Example 3.3: simultaneous causality. As a third example, consider the frequently referenced model from Duncan et al. (1971). In this model, illustrated in Figure 3.2, characteristics of a respondent and a

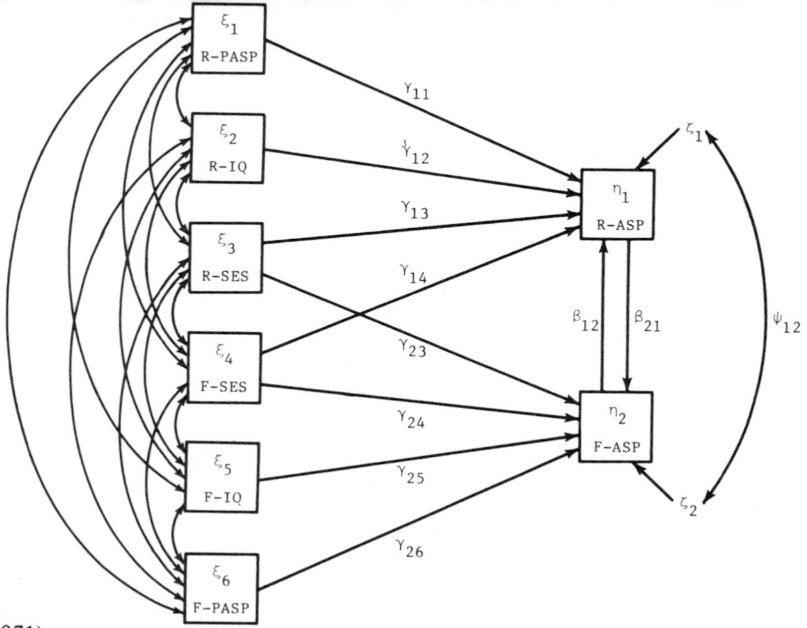

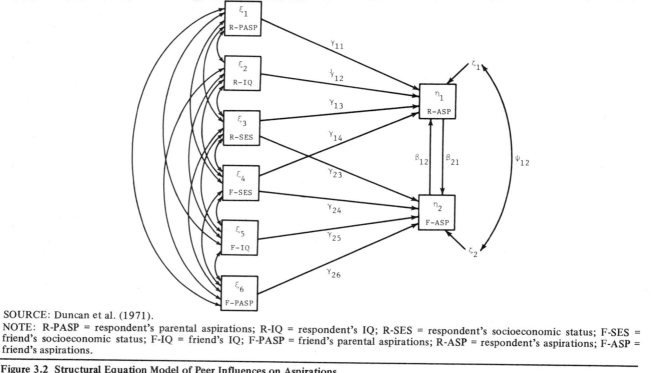

SOURCE: Duncan et al. (1971).

NOTE: R-PASP = respondent's parental aspirations; R-IQ = respondent's IQ; R-SES = respondent's socioeconomic status; F-SES = friend's socioeconomic status; F-IQ = friend's IQ; F-PASP = friend's parental aspirations; R-ASP = respondent's aspirations; F-ASP = friend's aspirations.

Figure 3.2 Structural Equation Model of Peer Influences on Aspirations

respondent's friend are used to predict the aspirations of the respondent and the respondent's friend. In the original model, two indicators of aspirations were used: occupational aspirations and educational aspirations. For the purposes of this chapter a single indicator, educational aspirations, is used. η_1 is the respondent's educational aspirations, and η_2 is the respondent's friend's educational aspirations. There are six exogenous variables. For the respondent, ξ_1 is a measure of the parents' aspirations for their child; ξ_2 is a measure of intelligence (hereafter referred to as IQ); and ξ_3 is a measure of SES. For the respondent's friend, ξ_6 is a measure of the parents' aspirations; ξ_5 is a measure of IQ; and ξ_4 is a measure of SES.

The structural equations for this model are

$$\begin{bmatrix} \eta_1 \\ \eta_2 \end{bmatrix} = \begin{bmatrix} \underline{0} & \beta_{12} \\ \beta_{21} & \underline{0} \end{bmatrix} \begin{bmatrix} \eta_1 \\ \eta_2 \end{bmatrix} + \begin{bmatrix} \gamma_{11} & \gamma_{12} & \gamma_{13} & \gamma_{14} & \underline{0} & \underline{0} \\ \underline{0} & \underline{0} & \gamma_{23} & \gamma_{24} & \gamma_{25} & \gamma_{26} \end{bmatrix} \begin{bmatrix} \xi_1 \\ \xi_2 \\ \xi_3 \\ \xi_4 \\ \xi_5 \\ \xi_6 \end{bmatrix} + \begin{bmatrix} \zeta_1 \\ \zeta_2 \end{bmatrix}$$

Thus, the respondent's aspirations (η_1) are assumed to be affected by the exogenous variables: his parents' aspirations (ξ_1), his IQ (ξ_2), his SES (ξ_3), and the SES of his friend (ξ_4) (i.e., $\gamma_{11} \neq 0$, $\gamma_{12} \neq 0$, $\gamma_{13} \neq 0$, and $\gamma_{14} \neq 0$; and $\gamma_{15} = \gamma_{16} = 0$). In the same way, the respondent's friend's aspirations (η_2) are assumed to be affected by his parents' aspirations (ξ_6), his IQ (ξ_5), his SES (ξ_4), and his friend's SES (ξ_3) (i.e., $\gamma_{23} \neq 0$, $\gamma_{24} \neq 0$, $\gamma_{25} \neq 0$, and $\gamma_{26} \neq 0$; and $\gamma_{21} = \gamma_{22} = 0$). Further, the respondents and friends are assumed to be mutually affected by one another's aspirations. Thus the respondent's aspirations (η_1) are affected by the respondent's friend's aspirations (η_2), and the respondent's friend's aspirations are affected by the respondent's aspirations (i.e., $\beta_{12} \neq 0$ and $\beta_{21} \neq 0$).

Finally, it is assumed that the errors in equations predicting respondent's aspirations are correlated with the errors in equations predicting the respondent's friend's aspirations:

$$\boldsymbol{\Psi} = \begin{bmatrix} \psi_{11} & \psi_{12} \\ \psi_{21} & \psi_{22} \end{bmatrix}$$

This might be caused by the exclusion of variables that jointly affect the respondent's and the friend's aspirations. //

The Covariance Structure

The covariances among the endogenous variables can be defined in terms of equation 3.1, the covariances among the exogenous variables ($\boldsymbol{\Phi}$), and the covariances among the errors in equations ($\boldsymbol{\Psi}$). Since $\ddot{\mathbf{B}}$ is assumed to be nonsingular, equation 3.2 can be multiplied by $\ddot{\mathbf{B}}^{-1}$: $\ddot{\mathbf{B}}^{-1}\ddot{\mathbf{B}}\boldsymbol{\eta} = \ddot{\mathbf{B}}^{-1}\boldsymbol{\Gamma\xi} + \ddot{\mathbf{B}}^{-1}\boldsymbol{\zeta}$, or more simply,

$$\boldsymbol{\eta} = \ddot{\mathbf{B}}^{-1}\boldsymbol{\Gamma\xi} + \ddot{\mathbf{B}}^{-1}\boldsymbol{\zeta} \qquad [3.4]$$

Equation 3.4 is referred to as the *reduced form* of the structural equation model, since structural relationships are reduced to a set of equations in which the endogenous variables are functions only of the exogenous variables and the errors in equations.

Since it was assumed that $E(\boldsymbol{\eta}) = \mathbf{0}$, the covariance matrix for $\boldsymbol{\eta}$ is equal to $E(\boldsymbol{\eta\eta}')$. Using the reduced form equation 3.4 allows us to write

$$\begin{aligned} \text{COV}(\boldsymbol{\eta}) &= E(\boldsymbol{\eta\eta}') = E\left[(\ddot{\mathbf{B}}^{-1}\boldsymbol{\Gamma\xi} + \ddot{\mathbf{B}}^{-1}\boldsymbol{\zeta})(\ddot{\mathbf{B}}^{-1}\boldsymbol{\Gamma\xi} + \ddot{\mathbf{B}}^{-1}\boldsymbol{\zeta})'\right] \\ &= E[(\ddot{\mathbf{B}}^{-1}\boldsymbol{\Gamma\xi\xi}'\boldsymbol{\Gamma}'\ddot{\mathbf{B}}'^{-1}) + (\ddot{\mathbf{B}}^{-1}\boldsymbol{\Gamma\xi\zeta}'\ddot{\mathbf{B}}'^{-1}) + \\ &\quad (\ddot{\mathbf{B}}^{-1}\boldsymbol{\zeta\xi}'\boldsymbol{\Gamma}'\ddot{\mathbf{B}}'^{-1}) + (\ddot{\mathbf{B}}^{-1}\boldsymbol{\zeta\zeta}'\ddot{\mathbf{B}}'^{-1})] \end{aligned}$$

Distributing the expectation operator, making use of the assumption that $E(\boldsymbol{\xi\zeta}') = \mathbf{0}$, and using the definitions of $\boldsymbol{\Phi}$ and $\boldsymbol{\Psi}$, it follows that

$$\begin{aligned} \text{COV}(\boldsymbol{\eta}) &= \ddot{\mathbf{B}}^{-1}\boldsymbol{\Gamma\Phi\Gamma}'\ddot{\mathbf{B}}'^{-1} + \ddot{\mathbf{B}}^{-1}\boldsymbol{\Psi}\ddot{\mathbf{B}}'^{-1} \\ &= \ddot{\mathbf{B}}^{-1}(\boldsymbol{\Gamma\Phi\Gamma}' + \boldsymbol{\Psi})\ddot{\mathbf{B}}'^{-1} \end{aligned}$$

Thus the covariances among the endogenous variables are defined in terms of the structural parameters $\boldsymbol{\Gamma}$ and $\ddot{\mathbf{B}}$, and the covariances among the exogenous variables and among the errors in equations.

The covariances among the ξ's and η's are derived similarly. Since $E(\boldsymbol{\xi}) = \mathbf{0}$ and $E(\boldsymbol{\eta}) = \mathbf{0}$, $\text{COV}(\boldsymbol{\eta},\boldsymbol{\xi}) = E(\boldsymbol{\eta\xi}')$. Substituting the reduced form $\ddot{\mathbf{B}}^{-1}\boldsymbol{\Gamma\xi} + \ddot{\mathbf{B}}^{-1}\boldsymbol{\zeta}$ for $\boldsymbol{\eta}$,

$$\begin{aligned} \text{COV}(\boldsymbol{\eta},\boldsymbol{\xi}) = E(\boldsymbol{\eta\xi}') &= E[(\ddot{\mathbf{B}}^{-1}\boldsymbol{\Gamma\xi} + \ddot{\mathbf{B}}^{-1}\boldsymbol{\zeta})\boldsymbol{\xi}'] \\ &= E[\ddot{\mathbf{B}}^{-1}\boldsymbol{\Gamma\xi\xi}' + \ddot{\mathbf{B}}^{-1}\boldsymbol{\zeta\xi}'] \\ &= \ddot{\mathbf{B}}^{-1}\boldsymbol{\Gamma\Phi} \end{aligned}$$

with the last equality following from the assumption that $E(\boldsymbol{\zeta\xi}') = \mathbf{0}$ and the definition $E(\boldsymbol{\xi\xi}') = \boldsymbol{\Phi}$.

These results allow us to define the (r+s × r+s) covariance matrix $\boldsymbol{\Sigma}$, containing the variances and covariances among the η's and ξ's:

$$\boldsymbol{\Sigma} = \left[\begin{array}{c|c} \text{COV}(\boldsymbol{\eta}) & \text{COV}(\boldsymbol{\eta},\boldsymbol{\xi}) \\ \hline \text{COV}(\boldsymbol{\xi},\boldsymbol{\eta}) & \text{COV}(\boldsymbol{\xi}) \end{array}\right] = \left[\begin{array}{c|c} \ddot{\mathbf{B}}^{-1}(\boldsymbol{\Gamma\Phi\Gamma}' + \boldsymbol{\Psi})\ddot{\mathbf{B}}'^{-1} & \ddot{\mathbf{B}}^{-1}\boldsymbol{\Gamma\Phi} \\ \hline \boldsymbol{\Phi\Gamma}'\ddot{\mathbf{B}}'^{-1} & \boldsymbol{\Phi} \end{array}\right] \quad [3.5]$$

$\boldsymbol{\Sigma}$ has been defined in terms of the structural parameters in $\mathbf{B}$ and $\boldsymbol{\Gamma}$, and the covariances contained in $\boldsymbol{\Phi}$ and $\boldsymbol{\Psi}$. Constraints imposed upon the structural parameters and upon the covariances restrict the values that $\boldsymbol{\Sigma}$ can assume. In practice $\boldsymbol{\Sigma}$ is unknown, but sample estimates of the covariances, contained in the matrix $\mathbf{S}$, are known. The process of estimation involves finding values of $\mathbf{B}$, $\boldsymbol{\Gamma}$, $\boldsymbol{\Phi}$, and $\boldsymbol{\Psi}$ that produce a covariance matrix according to equation 3.5 that is as close as possible to the observed covariance matrix $\mathbf{S}$.

Types of Structural Equation Models

In the structural equation model procedures for proving identification and for estimating parameters depend on the forms of $\mathbf{B}$ and $\boldsymbol{\Psi}$. Three forms of $\mathbf{B}$ need to be distinguished.

(1) $\mathbf{B}$ is a diagonal matrix, in which case endogenous variables are affected by exogenous variables, but not by endogenous variables.
(2) $\mathbf{B}$ is a triangular matrix, in which case endogenous variables can affect one another, but if η_j affects η_i, then η_i does not affect η_j.[2] That is, if $\beta_{ij} \neq 0$, then $\beta_{ji} = 0$.
(3) $\mathbf{B}$ has unrestricted elements above and below the diagonal. This allows any two endogenous variable to simultaneously affect one another. Thus, if η_j affects η_i, η_i can also affect η_j. If β_{ij} is not restricted to zero, β_{ji} may or may not be restricted to zero.

Two forms of $\boldsymbol{\Psi}$ are of concern.

(1) $\boldsymbol{\Psi}$ is diagonal. In this case, all of the errors in equations are uncorrelated. $\psi_{ij} = \psi_{ji} = 0$ for all $i \neq j$.
(2) $\boldsymbol{\Psi}$ is a symmetric, nondiagonal matrix. The errors in equation for at least two equations are correlated. That is, there is at least one $\psi_{ij} = \psi_{ji}$ that is not restricted to equal zero.

These forms of $\mathbf{B}$ and $\boldsymbol{\Psi}$ allow for six types of models.

Type 1. In the simplest case, both **B** and **Ψ** are restricted to be diagonal. For a single equation this corresponds to the multiple regression model. Example 3.1 above illustrates this case. If there is more than one equation, the information in one equation is of no use in identifying or estimating the parameters in the other equations. Each equation must be treated individually as a simple multiple regression.

Type 2. For this type of model no endogenous variable affects any other endogenous variable (i.e., **B** is diagonal), but the equations are related since the error in one equation is correlated with the error in another equation (i.e., an off-diagonal element of **Ψ** is not restricted to zero). When the exogenous variables in one equation are completely different from those in another equation, this corresponds to "seemingly unrelated regressions" (see Kmenta, 1971: 517-529).

Type 3. When **B** is triangular, an endogenous variable can affect another endogenous variable, but there is no simultaneous causality. If η_i affects η_j ($\beta_{ji} \neq 0$), η_j does not affect η_i ($\beta_{ij} = 0$). When this form of **B** is combined with a diagonal **Ψ**, the model is called recursive. The **B** matrix in Example 3.2 is triangular. In the first specification of **Ψ**, **Ψ** is assumed to be diagonal; hence the model is recursive.

Type 4. This case differs from the recursive model in that **Ψ** is not diagonal. As with the recursive model, **B** is assumed to be triangular. Models of this form commonly occur in panel models in which errors at the same time are correlated, or errors in equations for the same variable over time are correlated. In the second specifications of Model 3.2, **Ψ** is not diagonal and even though **B** is triangular, the model is not recursive.

Type 5. While models with simultaneous causality (i.e., **B** is not triangular or diagonal) are generally assumed to have errors correlated across equations (i.e., **Ψ** is not diagonal), this is not necessarily the case. If it can be justified that the errors in equations are uncorrelated, **Ψ** is diagonal regardless of the form of **B**. In some formulations of Example 3.3 this has been assumed.

Type 6. When simultaneous causality is present and errors in equations are correlated, Type 6 occurs. This model has been studied extensively by econometricians, and is referred to as a system of simultaneous equations, a nonrecursive model, an integrated structure, or a general interdependent system. Example 3.3 is an example of this type of model.

With these types of models in mind, it is possible to consider the issues of identification and estimation.

Identification

If a structural equation model is not identified, an infinite number of sets of parameters could generate the observed data. The researcher has no way to choose among the various solutions since each is equally valid or, if you wish, invalid. Identification can be obtained by imposing restrictions on **B**, **Γ**, and **Ψ**. Identification occurs if all but one set of parameters are excluded from consideration because they violate constraints imposed on the parameters being estimated.

The unrestricted structural equation model (i.e., no constraints on **B**, **Γ**, and **Ψ**) is unidentified. (See Wonnacott and Wonnacott [1979: 462] for a proof of this.) When **B** and **Ψ** have certain forms, the resulting models are always identified. Specifically, unrelated multiple regressions (Type 1), seemingly unrelated regressions (Type 2), and recursive equation systems (Type 3) are always identified. Models of Types 4 through 6 are unidentified unless sufficient additional restrictions are placed on **B**, **Γ**, and **Ψ**. Now let us turn to an examination of what types of restrictions are possible and how identification can be proven.

In simultaneous equation models (Type 6), identification is most often achieved by restricting selected elements of **B** and **Γ** to equal zero. If an element of **B** is restricted to zero, say β_{ij}, it means that the endogenous variable η_j does not affect the endogenous variable η_i. If an element of **Γ** is restricted to zero, say γ_{ij}, it means that exogenous variable ξ_j does not affect the endogenous variable η_i. Fisher (1966) has presented a powerful set of conditions for identification in terms of such exclusion restrictions. (See Wonnacott and Wonnacott [1979: 461-473] for a mathematically less demanding presentation of these conditions.)

The simplest condition to test is the *order condition*. It states that if an equation in a system of equations is identified, it must be true that the number of excluded variables in the equation is greater than or equal to the number of equations in the system minus one. Or in terms of constraints on **B** and **Γ**, the number of coefficients fixed to zero in a given row of **B** and **Γ** must be greater than or equal to the number of equations minus one. This is a necessary condition. If it is not true, the equation is not identified and cannot be estimated. If the condition is true, the model may or may not be identified. An example illustrates this condition.

Example 3.3: the order condition. The Duncan, Haller, and Portes model is a typical simultaneous equation system. The matrices of structural coefficients are

$$\mathbf{B} = \begin{bmatrix} \underline{0} & \beta_{12} \\ \beta_{21} & \underline{0} \end{bmatrix}$$

and

$$\mathbf{\Gamma} = \begin{bmatrix} \gamma_{11} & \gamma_{12} & \gamma_{13} & \gamma_{14} & \underline{0} & \underline{0} \\ \underline{0} & \underline{0} & \gamma_{23} & \gamma_{24} & \gamma_{25} & \gamma_{26} \end{bmatrix}$$

In row 1 of $\mathbf{\Gamma}$, there are two excluded variables: ξ_5 and ξ_6 are assumed not to affect η_1, as indicated by the constraints $\gamma_{15} = \gamma_{16} = 0$. Thus the number of excluded variables in the equation for η_1 is greater than the number of equations minus one: $2 > 1$, and the order condition for identification is satisfied. In the same way, two variables are excluded from the equation for η_2, and the necessary condition is also satisfied. //

A necessary and sufficient condition for identification is the *rank condition.* To state this condition, define $\ddot{\mathbf{B}}^{\#}$ as the matrix formed by excluding the row of $\ddot{\mathbf{B}}$ for the equation being considered, and deleting all columns for which there is not a zero in the excluded row. $\mathbf{\Gamma}^{\#}$ is defined by similar operations on $\mathbf{\Gamma}$. An equation is identified if and only if the rank of $[\ddot{\mathbf{B}}^{\#} | \mathbf{\Gamma}^{\#}]$, the matrix formed by joining $\ddot{\mathbf{B}}^{\#}$ and $\mathbf{\Gamma}^{\#}$, equals the number of equations minus one.[3] While this condition is often ignored in practice, this can be unwise. Even though the rank of $[\ddot{\mathbf{B}}^{\#} | \mathbf{\Gamma}^{\#}]$ cannot generally be known since the values of $\ddot{\mathbf{B}}$ and $\mathbf{\Gamma}$ are unknown (recall, they are to be estimated if the model is identified), it can sometimes be known that the rank is less than the number of equations minus one and, hence, that a given equation is not identified.

Example 3.3: the rank condition. To test the rank condition for the equation for η_1, first construct $\ddot{\mathbf{B}}^{\#}$ and $\mathbf{\Gamma}^{\#}$ by crossing out the appropriate elements of $\ddot{\mathbf{B}}$ and $\mathbf{\Gamma}$:

$$\ddot{\mathbf{B}}^{\#} = \begin{bmatrix} \cancel{\underline{1}} & -\cancel{\beta_{12}} \\ -\cancel{\beta_{21}} & \cancel{\underline{1}} \end{bmatrix}$$

and

$$\mathbf{\Gamma}^{\#} = \begin{bmatrix} \gamma_{11} & \gamma_{12} & \gamma_{13} & \gamma_{14} & \underline{0} & \underline{0} \\ \underline{0} & \underline{0} & \gamma_{23} & \gamma_{24} & \gamma_{25} & \gamma_{26} \end{bmatrix}$$

Accordingly, $[\ddot{\mathbf{B}}^{\#} \mid \mathbf{\Gamma}^{\#}]$ equals $[\gamma_{25}\ \gamma_{26}]$. The rank of $[\ddot{\mathbf{B}}^{\#} \mid \mathbf{\Gamma}^{\#}]$ will equal one unless both γ_{25} and γ_{26} are exactly equal to zero in the population. While this cannot be known with certainly, it is unlikely, and we can reasonably conclude that the equation for η_1 is identified. The rank condition can be applied to the equation for η_2 in the same fashion. //

Example 3.2: the rank and order conditions. Wheaton's (1978) model (see Figure 3.1 and equation 3.3) is a typical panel model with errors in equations for the same time period being correlated. As described earlier, **B** is triangular, and if we assume that $\mathbf{\Psi}$ is diagonal, the model is recursive and, consequently, is identified. If $\mathbf{\Psi}$ is assumed to be symmetric but not diagonal, the model is not recursive even though **B** is triangular, and the model is not necessarily identified. To test for identification, the order condition can be applied:

Dependent Variable	Number of Excluded Variables	? $\geq$	Number of Equations Minus One
η_1	4	yes	4
η_2	3	no	4
η_3	2	no	4
η_4	1	no	4
η_5	1	no	4

The equations for η_2 through η_5 are not identified. To determine if the equation for η_1 is identified, the rank condition must be checked. First, consider the matrix $[\ddot{\mathbf{B}}^{\#} \mid \mathbf{\Gamma}^{\#}]$, where crosses indicate elements to be deleted:

$$[\ddot{\mathbf{B}}^{\#} \mid \mathbf{\Gamma}^{\#}] = \left[\begin{array}{ccccc|c} 1 & \underline{0} & \underline{0} & \underline{0} & \underline{0} & \gamma_{11} \\ \beta_{21} & \underline{1} & \underline{0} & \underline{0} & \underline{0} & \gamma_{21} \\ \beta_{31} & \beta_{32} & \underline{1} & \underline{0} & \underline{0} & \gamma_{31} \\ \beta_{41} & \beta_{42} & \beta_{43} & \underline{1} & \underline{0} & \gamma_{41} \\ \beta_{51} & \beta_{52} & \beta_{53} & \underline{0} & \underline{1} & \gamma_{51} \end{array}\right] = \begin{bmatrix} \underline{1} & \underline{0} & \underline{0} & \underline{0} \\ \beta_{32} & \underline{1} & \underline{0} & \underline{0} \\ \beta_{42} & \beta_{43} & \underline{1} & \underline{0} \\ \beta_{52} & \beta_{53} & \underline{0} & \underline{1} \end{bmatrix}$$

The rank of $[\ddot{\mathbf{B}}^{\#} | \mathbf{\Gamma}^{\#}]$ is four; hence the equation for η_1 is identified without any restrictions on $\mathbf{\Psi}$. If restrictions are placed on $\mathbf{\Psi}$, the remaining equations may be identified, but the rank and order conditions cannot be used to determine it. //

In addition to exclusion restrictions, equality constraints (e.g., $\gamma_{23} = \gamma_{25}$), nonlinear restrictions, and restrictions on the covariances between errors in equations (e.g., $\Psi_{12} = \Psi_{21} = 0$) can also result in identification. When such restrictions are used, it is generally necessary to prove identification by solving the parameters of the model in terms of the variances and covariances of the observed variables, a necessary and sufficient condition for identification. An example of such a proof of identification is now given.

Example 3.2: identification. In the Wheaton model (see Figure 3.1), the assumption that $\mathbf{\Psi}$ is unrestricted is probably too harsh. Wheaton (1978) assumed that only the errors in equations predicting variables measured at the same point in time are correlated. The resulting $\mathbf{\Psi}$ is

$$\mathbf{\Psi} = \begin{bmatrix} \psi_{11} & \underline{0} & \underline{0} & \underline{0} & \underline{0} \\ \underline{0} & \psi_{22} & \psi_{23} & \underline{0} & \underline{0} \\ \underline{0} & \psi_{32} & \psi_{33} & \underline{0} & \underline{0} \\ \underline{0} & \underline{0} & \underline{0} & \psi_{44} & \psi_{45} \\ \underline{0} & \underline{0} & \underline{0} & \psi_{54} & \psi_{55} \end{bmatrix}$$

With these additional restrictions on $\mathbf{\Psi}$, the other equations in the model may be identified. To determine this, the parameters in $\mathbf{B}$, $\mathbf{\Gamma}$, and $\mathbf{\Psi}$ must be solved for in terms of the variances and covariances of the η's and ξ's.

The structural equations can be written as

$$\eta_1 = \gamma_{11}\xi_1 + \zeta_1 \qquad [3.6]$$

$$\eta_2 = \beta_{21}\eta_1 + \gamma_{21}\xi_1 + \zeta_2 \qquad [3.7]$$

$$\eta_3 = \beta_{31}\eta_1 + \beta_{32}\eta_2 + \gamma_{31}\xi_1 + \zeta_3 \qquad [3.8]$$

$$\eta_4 = \beta_{41}\eta_1 + \beta_{42}\eta_2 + \beta_{43}\eta_3 + \gamma_{41}\xi_1 + \zeta_4 \qquad [3.9]$$

$$\eta_5 = \beta_{51}\eta_1 + \beta_{52}\eta_2 + \beta_{53}\eta_3 + \gamma_{51}\xi_1 + \zeta_5 \qquad [3.10]$$

We know from the rank and order conditions that equation 3.6, hence γ_{11}, is identified. Multiplying equation 3.6 by itself and taking expectations (recall that the variables are measured as deviations from zero, and hence the expectation of a product equals a variance or a covariance), results in

$$E(\eta_1\eta_1) = VAR(\eta_1) = \gamma_{11}^2 VAR(\xi_1) + 2\gamma_{11}COV(\xi_1,\zeta_1) + \psi_{11}$$
$$= \gamma_{11}^2 VAR(\xi_1) + \psi_{11}$$

Since γ_{11} is identified, $VAR(\xi_1)$ is known, and $COV(\xi_1,\zeta_1)$ is assumed to equal zero, ψ_{11} can be solved for and hence is identified.

Equation 3.7 can be treated similarly. First, multiply equation 3.7 by ξ_1 and take expectations:

$$E(\eta_2\xi_1) = COV(\eta_2,\xi_1) = \beta_{21}COV(\eta_1,\xi_1) + \gamma_{21}COV(\xi_1, \xi_1) + COV(\zeta_2, \xi_1)$$
$$= \beta_{21}COV(\eta_1,\xi_1) + \gamma_{21}COV(\xi_1,\xi_1)$$

since $COV(\zeta_2,\xi_1)$ equals zero by assumption. Next, multiply equation 3.7 by η_1 and take expectations:

$$E(\eta_2\eta_1) = COV(\eta_2,\eta_1) = \beta_{21}COV(\eta_1,\eta_1) + \gamma_{21}COV(\xi_1,\eta_1) + COV(\zeta_2,\eta_1)$$

$COV(\zeta_2,\eta_1)$ equals zero, which can be seen by multiplying Equation 3.6 by ζ_2, and taking expectations: $E(\eta_1\zeta_2) = \gamma_{11}E(\xi_1\zeta_2) + E(\zeta_1\zeta_2)$, which equals zero since $E(\xi_1\zeta_2)$ and $E(\zeta_1\zeta_2) = \psi_{12}$ are assumed to equal zero. Now there are two equations in two unknowns:

$$COV(\eta_2,\xi_1) = \beta_{21}COV(\eta_1,\xi_1) + \gamma_{21}COV(\xi_1,\xi_1)$$
$$COV(\eta_2,\eta_1) = \beta_{21}COV(\eta_1,\eta_1) + \gamma_{21}COV(\xi_1,\eta_1)$$

The parameters β_{21} and γ_{21} can be easily solved for and hence are identified.

ψ_{22} can be proved identified by multiplying equation 3.7 by itself and taking expectations:

$$COV(\eta_2,\eta_2) = \beta_{21}^2 COV(\eta_1,\eta_1) + \gamma_{21}^2 COV(\xi_1,\xi_1) + \psi_{22} +$$
$$2\beta_{21}\gamma_{21}COV(\eta_1,\xi_1) + 2\beta_{21}COV(\eta_1,\zeta_2) + 2\gamma_{21}COV(\xi_1,\zeta_2)$$

Since the covariances with ζ_2 are assumed to equal zero, and all other parameters in the equation except for ψ_{22} are either known or are identified, ψ_{22} can be solved for and hence is identified.

With the restrictions currently imposed, equation 3.8 is not identified. Multiplying equation 3.8 by ξ_1, η_1, and η_2 and taking expectations:

$$\begin{aligned}
COV(\eta_3,\xi_1) &= \beta_{31}COV(\eta_1,\xi_1) + \beta_{32}COV(\eta_2,\xi_1)+ \\
&\quad \gamma_{31}COV(\xi_1,\xi_1) + COV(\zeta_3,\xi_1) \\
COV(\eta_3,\eta_1) &= \beta_{31}COV(\eta_1,\eta_1) + \beta_{32}COV(\eta_2,\eta_1)+ \\
&\quad \gamma_{31}COV(\xi_1,\eta_1) + COV(\zeta_3,\eta_1) \\
COV(\eta_3,\eta_2) &= \beta_{31}COV(\eta_1,\eta_2) + \beta_{32}COV(\eta_2,\eta_2)+ \\
&\quad \gamma_{31}COV(\xi_1,\eta_2) + COV(\zeta_3,\eta_2)
\end{aligned} \tag{3.11}$$

While $COV(\zeta_3,\eta_1)$ and $COV(\zeta_3,\xi_1)$ equal zero, $COV(\zeta_3,\eta_2) = \psi_{23}$ does not. Therefore, there are three equations in four unknowns (β_{31}, β_{32}, γ_{31}, and ψ_{23}), which cannot be solved uniquely.

Attempts to find a fourth equation in order to solve for the four unknowns cannot be successful, since each new equation introduces additional unknowns. For example,

$$\begin{aligned}
COV(\eta_3,\eta_3) &= \beta_{31}^2COV(\eta_1,\eta_1) + \beta_{32}^2COV(\eta_2,\eta_2) + \gamma_{31}^2COV(\xi_1,\xi_1)+ \\
&\quad \psi_{33}^2 + 2\beta_{31}\gamma_{31}COV(\eta_1,\xi_1) + 2\beta_{32}\gamma_{31}COV(\eta_2,\xi_1)+ \\
&\quad 2\beta_{32}\beta_{31}COV(\eta_1,\eta_2) + 2\gamma_{31}COV(\xi_1,\zeta_3) + 2\beta_{31}COV(\eta_1,\zeta_3)+ \\
&\quad 2\beta_{32}COV(\eta_2,\zeta_3)
\end{aligned}$$

While an additional equation has been added, so has the additional unidentified parameter ψ_{33}. Three equations that cannot be solved for four unknowns have been replaced by four equations that cannot be solved for five unknowns. Attempts to find other equations with which to solve for the parameters will be similarly thwarted by the introduction of additional, unidentified parameters. Accordingly, the model with the restrictions currently imposed is not identified, although equations 3.6 and 3.7 are identified.

Wheaton (1978) encountered the same unidentifiability of the structural component of the model he analyzed (even though he also had a measurement model). The restrictions he imposed to identify the model were that β_{32}, β_{41}, and β_{51} equal zero; that is, three of the causal paths among the endogenous variables were assumed to be absent. With these additional exclusion restrictions, the identification of the model can be readily demonstrated.

Equation set 3.11 now contains three equations in three unknowns that can be solved for. Proceeding in a similar fashion, the other parameters in the model can also be shown to be identified. //

For an additional example of how models with constraints on **Ψ** can be proved to be identified, see Hanushek and Jackson (1977: 271-276).

Estimation

Once a structural equation model is known to be identified, estimation can proceed. If an attempt is made to estimate a model that is not identified, the estimates of the unidentified parameters are meaningless.

As with identification, the method of estimation depends on the form of the **B** and **Ψ** matrices. For unrelated multiple regression (Type 1), ordinary least squares is optimal. If **B** is diagonal, but **Ψ** is not (Type 2), the method of estimation depends on the exogenous variables. If the exogenous variables are identical in all equations, ordinary least squares provides unbiased and efficient estimates. If the equations do not share variables, the case of seemingly unrelated regressions, ordinary least squares is unbiased and consistent, but not efficient. Generalized least squares provides efficient estimates in this case.[4] For recursive models (Type 3) ordinary least squares provides consistent and efficient estimates. If the model does not include lagged endogenous variables, ordinary least squares is also unbiased. Simultaneous equation systems in which there are no constraints on **Ψ**, can be estimated by a variety of methods: two-stage least squares, instrumental variables, limited information maximum likelihood, full information maximum likelihood, and three-stage least squares (among others).

Each of the types of models just described and their methods of estimation have received extended discussion in the econometrics literature. See Hanushek and Jackson (1977) for a relatively simple introduction, Kmenta (1971) for a more thorough and demanding treatment, and Malinvaud (1970) for a very demanding treatment that approaches estimation in the manner closest to what is used for the covariance structure model. These models can be estimated with a variety of commonly available software packages. It is beyond the scope of this discussion to review these methods. Rather, the focus is on applications that cannot be easily incorporated into standard statistical packages and that have been relatively neglected in the econometrics literature. For example, if **Ψ** has some but not all off-diagonal elements restricted to zero or if equality constraints have been imposed (both of which occur commonly in panel models), most regression packages cannot provide the desired estimates. In such cases, the software developed for the covariance structure model provides the most convenient method of estimation.

Before discussing specific methods, a distinction between full information and limited information techniques—what are sometimes referred to as single equation methods versus system methods—is necessary (see Hanushek and Jackson, 1977: 277-278). A limited information technique estimates each equation separately without using information on restrictions in other equations. Full information techniques estimate the entire system of equations simultaneously and have the advantage that the estimation of each parameter utilizes the information provided by the entire system. Such methods are statistically more efficient. On the other hand, full information techniques are limited by their advantages. Since the estimation of each parameter is dependent upon every other parameter in the model, estimates of each parameter are affected by misspecification in any equation of the model. Limited information methods, while less efficient, estimate each equation separately; hence estimation of one equation is not affected by misspecification in other equations. Accordingly, when model specification is uncertain, limited information methods are preferred.

Estimation using software for the covariance structure model can be thought of as follows.[5] The researcher begins with the *sample* covariance matrix **S**. Diagonal elements are variances of the observed variables, and off-diagonal elements are covariances. If the data are standardized, **S** contains the correlations among the observed variables. It is useful to think of **S** as a partitioned matrix:

$$\mathbf{S} = \left[\begin{array}{c|c} \text{Sample estimates of covariances among } \eta\text{'s} & \text{Sample estimates of covariances between } \eta\text{'s \& } \xi\text{'s} \\ \hline \text{Sample estimates of covariances between } \xi\text{'s \& } \eta\text{'s} & \text{Sample estimates of covariances among } \xi\text{'s} \end{array}\right]$$

An estimate of the *population* covariance matrix $\mathbf{\Sigma}$ is defined in terms of estimates of $\ddot{\mathbf{B}}$, $\mathbf{\Gamma}$, $\mathbf{\Phi}$, and $\mathbf{\Psi}$ (see equation 3.5):

$$\hat{\Sigma} = \left[\begin{array}{c|c} \widehat{\text{COV}}(\boldsymbol{\eta}) & \widehat{\text{COV}}(\boldsymbol{\eta},\boldsymbol{\xi}) \\ \hline \widehat{\text{COV}}(\boldsymbol{\xi},\boldsymbol{\eta}) & \widehat{\text{COV}}(\boldsymbol{\xi}) \end{array}\right] = \left[\begin{array}{c|c} \hat{\ddot{\mathbf{B}}}^{-1}(\hat{\mathbf{\Gamma}}\hat{\mathbf{\Phi}}\hat{\mathbf{\Gamma}}' + \hat{\mathbf{\Psi}})\hat{\ddot{\mathbf{B}}}'^{-1} & \hat{\ddot{\mathbf{B}}}^{-1}\hat{\mathbf{\Gamma}}\hat{\mathbf{\Phi}} \\ \hline \hat{\mathbf{\Phi}}\hat{\mathbf{\Gamma}}'\hat{\ddot{\mathbf{B}}}'^{-1} & \hat{\mathbf{\Phi}} \end{array}\right]$$

where the ^ indicates that the matrices contain estimates of population parameters. These estimates must satisfy the constraints that have been imposed on the model. Estimation involves finding values of $\hat{\mathbf{B}}$, $\hat{\mathbf{\Gamma}}$, $\hat{\mathbf{\Phi}}$, and $\hat{\mathbf{\Psi}}$ that generate an estimated covariance matrix $\hat{\mathbf{\Sigma}}$ that is as close as possible to the sample covariance matrix **S**. This is done by considering all possible sets of matrices having the dimensions of the matrices $\ddot{\mathbf{B}}$, $\mathbf{\Gamma}$, $\mathbf{\Phi}$, and $\mathbf{\Psi}$. Many of these possible matrices must be excluded from consideration because they do not incorporate the constraints imposed on the parameters. Let $\ddot{\mathbf{B}}^*$, $\mathbf{\Gamma}^*$, $\mathbf{\Phi}^*$, and $\mathbf{\Psi}^*$ be any matrices that incorporate the imposed constraints. This set of matrices defines a matrix $\mathbf{\Sigma}^*$ according to the formula

$$\mathbf{\Sigma}^* = \left[\begin{array}{c|c} \mathrm{COV}(\eta)^* & \mathrm{COV}(\eta,\xi)^* \\ \hline \mathrm{COV}(\xi,\eta)^* & \mathrm{COV}(\xi)^* \end{array}\right] = \left[\begin{array}{c|c} \ddot{\mathbf{B}}^{*-1}(\mathbf{\Gamma}^*\mathbf{\Phi}^*\mathbf{\Gamma}^{*\prime} + \mathbf{\Psi}^*)\ddot{\mathbf{B}}^{*\prime-1} & \ddot{\mathbf{B}}^{*-1}\mathbf{\Gamma}^*\mathbf{\Phi}^* \\ \hline \mathbf{\Phi}^*\mathbf{\Gamma}^{*\prime}\ddot{\mathbf{B}}^{*\prime-1} & \mathbf{\Phi}^* \end{array}\right]$$

If $\mathbf{\Sigma}^*$ is "close" to **S**, one might conclude that $\ddot{\mathbf{B}}^*$, $\mathbf{\Gamma}^*$, $\mathbf{\Phi}^*$, and $\mathbf{\Psi}^*$ are reasonable estimates of the population parameters. The problems of estimation are to measure how close $\mathbf{\Sigma}^*$ is to **S**, and to find the values of $\ddot{\mathbf{B}}^*$, $\mathbf{\Gamma}^*$, $\mathbf{\Phi}^*$, and $\mathbf{\Psi}^*$ that produce the $\mathbf{\Sigma}^*$ that is as close as possible to **S**.

A function that measures how close a given $\mathbf{\Sigma}^*$ is to the sample covariance matrix **S** is called a *fitting function.* A fitting function is designated as $F(\mathbf{S};\mathbf{\Sigma}^*)$, or to indicate that $\mathbf{\Sigma}^*$ is defined by $\mathbf{B}^*$, $\mathbf{\Gamma}^*$, $\mathbf{\Phi}^*$, and $\mathbf{\Psi}^*$, it may be written as $F(\mathbf{S};\mathbf{B}^*,\mathbf{\Gamma}^*,\mathbf{\Phi}^*,\mathbf{\Psi}^*)$. This function is defined over all possible $\mathbf{B}^*$, $\mathbf{\Gamma}^*$, $\mathbf{\Phi}^*$, and $\mathbf{\Psi}^*$ that satisfy the constraints on **B**, $\mathbf{\Gamma}$, $\mathbf{\Phi}$, and $\mathbf{\Psi}$. Those values of $\mathbf{B}^*$, $\mathbf{\Gamma}^*$, $\mathbf{\Phi}^*$, and $\mathbf{\Psi}^*$ that minimize the fitting function for a given **S** are the sample estimates of the population parameters and are designated as $\hat{\mathbf{B}}$, $\hat{\mathbf{\Gamma}}$, $\hat{\mathbf{\Phi}}$, and $\hat{\mathbf{\Psi}}$.

Three fitting functions are commonly used in software for the covariance structure model. These correspond to unweighted least squares (ULS), generalized least squares (GLS), and maximum likelihood (ML).

The ULS estimators of **B**, $\mathbf{\Gamma}$, $\mathbf{\Phi}$, and $\mathbf{\Psi}$ are those values that minimize the fitting function:

$$F_{\mathrm{ULS}}(\mathbf{S};\mathbf{\Sigma}^*) = \mathrm{tr}[(\mathbf{S} - \mathbf{\Sigma}^*)^2]$$

where "tr" is the trace operator indicating the sum of the diagonal elements of a matrix. The ULS estimator can be shown to be consistent without making any assumptions about the distribution of the observed variables (Bentler and Weeks, 1979). This means that for large samples, ULS is approximately unbiased. Not having to make distributional assumptions about the observed variables is an advantage, but it is offset by two limitations. First, there are no statistical tests associated with ULS estimation. Second, ULS estimators have a property known as *scale dependency,* a concept discussed in *CFA*.

The fitting function for GLS is more complex, with differences between **S** and $\boldsymbol{\Sigma}^*$ being weighted by elements of $\mathbf{S}^{-1}$ (see Jöreskog and Goldberger, 1972 for details). The GLS fitting function is

$$F_{GLS}(\mathbf{S};\boldsymbol{\Sigma}^*) = \mathrm{tr}[(\mathbf{S} - \boldsymbol{\Sigma}^*)\mathbf{S}^{-1}]^2$$

The ML estimator minimizes the fitting function defined as

$$F_{ML}(\mathbf{S};\boldsymbol{\Sigma}^*) = \mathrm{tr}(\boldsymbol{\Sigma}^{*-1}\mathbf{S}) + [\log|\boldsymbol{\Sigma}^*| - \log|\mathbf{S}|] - (r + s)$$

where $\log|\boldsymbol{\Sigma}^*|$ is the log of the determinant of $\boldsymbol{\Sigma}^*$. If $\boldsymbol{\xi}$ and $\boldsymbol{\eta}$ have a multivariate normal distribution, both GLS and ML have desirable asymptotic properties. The ML estimator is approximately unbiased, has as small a sampling variance as any other estimator, and is approximately normally distributed. This means that if the assumptions about the distribution of $\boldsymbol{\xi}$ and $\boldsymbol{\eta}$ hold, as the sample size gets larger, (1) the expected values of the sample estimates get closer and closer to the true population parameters; (2) the variance of the sampling distribution of the ML estimators becomes as small as possible with any estimator; and (3) the sampling distribution of the estimators becomes normal. In the covariance structure model, GLS is asymptotically equivalent to ML (Lee, 1977; Browne, 1974). Both methods of estimation are scale invariant and have desirable properties for statistical testing.

Note that these are asymptotic properties. Strictly speaking, they are justified only as the sample approaches an infinite size. An important practical question is, how large must a sample be in order to take advantage of the desirable asymptotic properties? Unfortunately, there is no definitive answer to this question, although Boomsma (1982) has obtained some results for the confirmatory factor model. (See *CFA* for details.) GLS and ML also require assumptions of normality, with GLS being justified under slightly less restrictive assumptions than ML (Browne, 1974). Unfortunately, very little is known about the effects of violations of the assumption of normality in our model.

Practical Considerations

In general, none of these estimators (ULS, GLS, and ML) has closed form solutions. The values that minimize the fitting functions must be found by numerically searching over possible values of $\mathbf{B}$, $\mathbf{\Gamma}$, $\mathbf{\Phi}$, and $\mathbf{\Psi}$. Technical details on how the search is conducted need not concern us, although three practical problems are worth noting.

First, it is possible for search procedures to locate what is called a "local minimum." This is a value of the fitting function that appears to be the smallest possible when actually there are other smaller values. Such occurrences are thought to be rare (Jöreskog and Sörbom, 1981: I.31).

Second, the values of the parameters that minimize the fitting function may be outside the range of feasible values. For example, a variance may be estimated to be negative or a correlation to be greater than one. Such occurrences are thought to result from misspecified models or insufficiently large sample sizes. This issue is discussed in more detail in *CFA*.

Third, numerical searches can be costly in computer time. The time required for estimating a given model is based on (1) the number of independent elements in the covariance matrix for the observed variables, (2) the number of parameters to be estimated, and (3) how close the start values are to the actual values of the estimates. Software estimating the covariance structure model requires start values for each parameter that is to be estimated. Start values are guesses that the user supplies, which are used to compute the first $\mathbf{\Sigma}^*$. The search proceeds by refining these initial guesses. The closer the start values, the easier it will be to find the final estimates. Choosing start values can be difficult, although the most recent version of LISREL (Jöreskog and Sörbom, 1981) has incorporated an algorithm for generating start values for most models.

The estimates obtained by ULS or GLS do not correspond to any commonly used methods of estimation for structural equation models and, hence, are not discussed further in this chapter. If assumptions of normality are made, the ML estimates correspond to full information maximum likelihood (FIML) estimates for structural equation models (see Theil, 1971: 524-525). If the assumptions of normality are not justified, full information maximum likelihood estimates are still justified since they are equivalent to the method of full information least generalized residual variance (see Jöreskog and Sörbom, 1981: III.53; Kmenta, 1971: 579). However, when assumptions of normality cannot be made, the statistical tests discussed below should be used with caution.

The most recent version of LISREL (Jöreskog and Sörbom, 1981) estimates start values. For structural equation models these initial estimates correspond to the well-known method of two-stage least squares

(Jöreskog and Sörbom, 1981: III.48), which provides limited information, consistent estimates of the parameters of the structural equation model.

Assessing Goodness of Fit

This section reviews the techniques for assessing goodness of fit that are available with software for the covariance structure model. A more detailed discussion is found in *CFA*. If a structural equation model is being studied which can be estimated with more traditional statistical packages (i.e., those without equality constraints or constraints on a $\boldsymbol{\Psi}$ that is not diagonal), additional methods of assessing the fit of a model can be employed. Extensive discussions of such techniques can be found in the econometric literature.

Examining values of the parameters. The first step is to consider the estimates of each individual parameter. Unreasonable values indicate that something is wrong with the model. The model may be misspecified, resulting in biased estimates. The model may not be identified, resulting in one of an infinite set of possible estimates. The sample may be so small that estimates are imprecise and asymptotic properties cannot be applied. The input data may be an inappropriate pairwise correlations or covariance matrix; or, the control cards for the program being used may be incorrectly coded.

Variances of the estimates. With GLS and ML the covariance matrix for the estimates is computed. With the variances of the estimates, z-tests of individual parameters can be performed to test the hypothesis that a parameter is equal to some fixed value. Such tests are identical to those generally employed in multiple regression. Recall that these tests are based on assumptions of normality and must be employed with caution if such assumptions are unrealistic.

Chi-square goodness-of-fit tests. A chi-square test can be computed with ML and GLS estimation to test the hypothesis H_0 that the observed covariance matrix was generated by the hypothesized model, against the alternative hypothesis H_1 that the covariance matrix is an unrestricted covariance matrix. Rejecting this hypothesis indicates that the model does not adequately reproduce the observed covariance matrix **S**. Degrees of freedom (df) for the chi-square test can be computed as follows:

df = the number of independent parameters under H_1 minus the number of independent parameters under H_0;

or more specifically,

df = the number of independent elements in $\mathbf{\Sigma}$ minus the number of independent elements in $\mathbf{B}$, $\mathbf{\Gamma}$, $\mathbf{\Phi}$, and $\mathbf{\Psi}$.

If a model is just-identified, the number of independent elements in $\mathbf{\Sigma}$ will equal the number of independent parameters in $\mathbf{B}$, $\mathbf{\Gamma}$, $\mathbf{\Phi}$, and $\mathbf{\Psi}$, resulting in a chi-square of zero with zero degrees of freedom. Accordingly, the chi-square test will not be of value in assessing the fit of a just-identified model.[6]

Difference of chi-square tests. While F-tests are generally used in multiple regression to test simultaneous hypotheses (Wonnacott and Wonnacott, 1979: 184-186), a difference of chi-square test can be used for the same purpose when estimating regression models with programs for the covariance structure model. If model M_1 with X_1^2 and df_1 is nested in M_2 with X_2^2 and df_2, the hypothesis that the parameters restricted in M_1 but not in M_2 are equal to zero can be tested by the difference of chi-square test: $X^2 = X_1^2 - X_2^2$ with $df = df_1 - df_2$.

The coefficient of determination. In classical regression theory (see Wonnacott and Wonnacott, 1979: 180-181), the coefficient of determination is defined as the percentage of the variation in the dependent variable that is explained by the regression. The coefficient of determination for the equation predicting η_i can be defined as

$$R^2 = 1 - \frac{VAR(\zeta_i)}{VAR(\eta_i)}$$

where ζ_i is the error in the equation for η_i. Care should be used in applying the coefficient of determination to multiple equation systems, since what is accounted for as explained variation in η_i can include variation explained by errors in other equations.

As Example 3.2 will illustrate, it is possible to have a large R^2 and a chi-square that indicates an unacceptable level of fit. This corresponds to the situation in multiple regression where the R^2 is large, but a significant increase in the R^2 can be obtained if additional explanatory variables are included in the model. Equivalently, a significant improvement in fit can be obtained by relaxing constraints on parameters in the model.

Modification indices. If the fit of the model is not adequate, it is possible to improve the fit by adding additional parameters to the model. One approach to selecting which parameters to add is based on partial derivatives of the fitting function with respect to each of the parameters that have been fixed (Sörbom, 1975). The derivative indicates how rapidly the fitting function, and hence the chi-square, will decrease if the parameter is freed. Use of the derivative is limited since a parameter with a large derivative may have a fixed value very close to the value that would be estimated if that parameter were freed. If this were the case, the total improvement in fit would be small. Jöreskog and Sörbom (1981: I.42) have proposed a modification index that remedies the problem. The index for a given fixed parameter is equal to the expected decrease in the chi-square if that parameter were freed. It is suggested that only one parameter be relaxed at a time, since freeing one parameter may reduce or eliminate the improvement in fit possible by freeing a second parameter. The parameter to be relaxed at each step should have the largest modification index, and should make substantive sense to relax. (See *CFA* for more details.)

Interpreting Structural Coefficients

The structural coefficients in **B** and **Γ** can be interpreted as direct effects on the endogenous variables. β_{ij} indicates that a unit change in the endogenous variable η_j results in a change of β_{ij} units in η_i, all other variables being held constant. Similarly, γ_{ij} indicates that a unit change in the exogenous variable ξ_j results in a change in η_i of γ_{ij} units, holding all other variables constant. If the variables have been standardized, the interpretations are adjusted accordingly. A standard deviation change in η_j results in a β_{ij} standard deviation change in η_i, all other variables being held constant; a standard deviation change in ξ_j results in a γ_{ij} standard deviation change in η_i, all other variables being held constant.

These interpretations assume that all other variables are being held constant. In practice, however, a change in a given exogenous variable is likely to be associated with a change in more than a single other variable. Consider Example 3.3: γ_{13} indicates that a unit change in respondent's SES (ξ_3) results in a direct change of γ_{13} units in respondent's aspirations (η_1), assuming that a change in ξ_3 is not associated with a change in any other variables that can affect η_1. But in this model a change in ξ_3 is assumed to cause a change in η_2 (via the direct effect on γ_{23}), and a change in η_2 is assumed to affect η_1 (via the direct effect β_{12}). Thus, a change in ξ_3 has both a direct effect on η_1 and additional, indirect effects when the other variables are not assumed to be held constant. Accordingly, the total effect on η_1 of a change in ξ_3 must include at least the direct effect of ξ_3 on η_1 and the indirect effect of ξ_3 that operates through

η_2. This example illustrates that in interpreting effects in a structural equation model it is necessary to distinguish between direct, indirect, and total effects.[7]

In the model $\boldsymbol{\eta} = \mathbf{B}\boldsymbol{\eta} + \boldsymbol{\Gamma}\boldsymbol{\xi} + \boldsymbol{\zeta}$, the direct effects of $\boldsymbol{\eta}$ on $\boldsymbol{\eta}$ are contained in $\mathbf{B}$, and the direct effects of $\boldsymbol{\xi}$ on $\boldsymbol{\eta}$ are contained in $\boldsymbol{\Gamma}$. Total effects of $\boldsymbol{\xi}$ on $\boldsymbol{\eta}$ are obtained from the reduced form equation $\boldsymbol{\eta} = (\mathbf{I} - \mathbf{B})^{-1}\boldsymbol{\Gamma}\boldsymbol{\xi} + (\mathbf{I} - \mathbf{B})^{-1}\boldsymbol{\zeta}$. If $\boldsymbol{\Pi}$ is defined as $\boldsymbol{\Pi} = (\mathbf{I} - \mathbf{B})^{-1}\boldsymbol{\Gamma}$, then π_{ij} indicates the total effect of a change in ξ_j on η_i. Total effects of η's on η's are more complex to derive since they must take into account the reciprocal effects among endogenous variables. In Example 3.3, a change in η_1 affects η_2 through β_{21}. The change in η_2 in turn affects η_1 through β_{12}, and so on. The resulting total effect of $\boldsymbol{\eta}$ on $\boldsymbol{\eta}$ is computed as $(\mathbf{I} - \mathbf{B})^{-1} - \mathbf{I}$. Indirect effects can be computed simply as the differences between total and direct effects. A detailed treatment of this topic and complete derivations can be found in Graff and Schmidt (1982), Fox (1980), and Jöreskog and Sörbom (1981).

To illustrate estimation and hypothesis testing in the structural equation model, Examples 3.2 and 3.3 are used. The reader is encouraged to replicate these examples using the data in the Appendix.

Example 3.3: estimation and hypothesis testing. In the form presented above, this model is a traditional simultaneous equation system that can be estimated by any of a number of methods of estimation. Table 3.2 presents estimates by the limited information methods of two-stage least squares (2SLS) and limited information maximum likelihood (LIML), and the full information methods of three-stage least squares (3SLS) and full information maximum likelihood (FIML). The first three methods were estimated using SAS's procedure SYSREG, and FIML was computed using LISREL V. While the full information estimates are most similar to each other and the limited information estimates are most similar to each other, estimates by all methods are very close.

Consider now the interpretation of the FIML coefficients in Table 3.2. The strongest direct effect on the respondent's educational aspirations (η_1) is the respondent's SES (ξ_3): A standard deviation increase in ξ_3 results in a direct increase of 0.277 ($= \hat{\gamma}_{13}$) standard deviations in η_1, all other variables being held constant. This effect is statistically significant at the .001 level for a one-tailed test. The direct effect does not represent the total effect of ξ_3 on η_1, since a change in ξ_3 also affects η_2, which in turn affects η_1. The total effect is somewhat larger, equaling 0.296. The effects of ξ_1 and ξ_2 are also statistically significant, but slightly weaker.

TABLE 3.2
Alternative Methods of Estimation for Structural Equation Model of Peer Influence on Aspirations (Model M_a)

	2SLS		*LIML*		*3SLS*		*FIML*	
Coefficient	*Effect*	*t*	*Effect*	*t*	*Effect*	*t*	*Effect*	*z*
β_{12}	0.158	1.39	0.158	1.37	0.157	1.38	0.157	1.38
γ_{11}	0.196	4.20	0.196	4.20	0.193	4.22	0.193	4.20
γ_{12}	0.252	4.86	0.252	4.86	0.254	4.97	0.254	5.00
γ_{13}	0.277	5.37	0.277	5.36	0.277	5.36	0.277	5.35
γ_{14}	0.050	0.83	0.050	0.83	0.050	0.83	0.050	0.83
β_{21}	0.240	1.90	0.240	1.90	0.238	1.89	0.239	1.91
γ_{23}	0.047	0.76	0.047	0.75	0.047	0.76	0.047	0.76
γ_{24}	0.254	5.33	0.254	5.33	0.250	5.27	0.251	5.21
γ_{25}	0.323	6.28	0.323	6.28	0.333	6.53	0.332	6.80
γ_{26}	0.201	4.58	0.201	4.58	0.189	4.40	0.189	4.32

NOTE: See Figure 3.2 or text for specific meanings of coefficients. All coefficients are standardized. 2SLS is two-stage least squares; LIML is limited information maximum likelihood; 3SLS is three-stage least squares; and FIML is full-information maximum likelihood. 2SLS, LIML, and 3SLS estimates were computed with the SAS procedure SYSREG. FIML estimates were computed with LISREL V.

Neither the direct effect of η_2 nor of ξ_4 is statistically significant. The overall fit of the model is statisfactory, with a chi-square of 1.88 with two degrees of freedom (prob = .39). See Table 3.3.

While the fit of M_a is satisfactory, it is instructive to consider whether the fit can be improved. In the equation for η_1, either the parameter γ_{15} or γ_{16} (but not both) could be freed and the resulting model would still be identified. Similarly, the parameter for γ_{21} or γ_{22} (but not both) could be freed. Since there is no substantive justification for including these effects, doing so is unjustified. Similarly, while additional exclusion constraints could be imposed (e.g., restricting γ_{14} to zero), there are theoretical reasons for including these variables.

The symmetry of the model suggests another approach. Each effect for the respondent corresponds to an effect for the respondent's friend. There is no reason to expect that corresponding effects for the friend and the respondent will be different. For example, the effect of the respondent's aspirations on the friend's aspirations should equal the effect of the

TABLE 3.3

FIML Estimates of Three Models for Peer Influences on Aspirations (Models M_a, M_b, and M_c)

	M_a		M_b		M_c	
Coefficient	*Effect*	*z*	*Effect*	*z*	*Effect*	*z*
β_{12}	0.157	1.38	0.194[a]	2.25	0.192[a]	2.24
γ_{11}	0.193	4.20	0.193	4.21	0.192[b]	6.01
γ_{12}	0.254	5.00	0.250	5.00	0.269[c]	8.13
γ_{13}	0.277	5.35	0.270	5.42	0.264[d]	7.40
γ_{14}	0.050	0.83	0.038	0.69	0.052[e]	1.20
β_{21}	0.239	1.91	0.194[a]	2.25	0.192[a]	2.24
γ_{23}	0.047	0.76	0.062	1.19	0.052[e]	1.20
γ_{24}	0.251	5.21	0.256	5.49	0.264[d]	7.40
γ_{25}	0.332	6.80	0.337	6.93	0.296[c]	8.13
γ_{26}	0.189	4.32	0.188	4.31	0.192[b]	6.01
Chi-square	1.88		2.12		4.28	
df	2		3		7	
prob	0.39		0.55		0.75	

NOTE: Roman letters indicate that coefficients are constrained to be equal. See Figure 3.2 or text for specific meanings of coefficients. All coefficients are standardized and estimated by FIML (full-information maximum likelihood). Estimates were computed with LISREL V.

friend's aspirations on the respondent's aspirations. This involves the constraint $\beta_{12} = \beta_{21}$ (see, for example, Jöreskog and Sörbom, 1981: III.88). This constraint is contained in model M_b of Table 3.3. The addition of this constraint adds one degree of freedom and increases the chi-square by 0.24. Assuming that a formal hypothesis test was appropriate (which it is not, given our exploratory search), the hypotheses H_0: $\beta_{12} = \beta_{21}$ could be tested with a difference of chi-square between the nested models M_a and M_b. The resulting chi-square of 0.24 with one degree of freedom indicates that the hypothesis cannot be rejected. The effect of imposing this constraint on β_{12} and β_{21} is as might be expected. The new estimates of $\beta_{12} = \beta_{21}$ are an "average" of those in model M_a, with an increase in their statistical significance.

In the same way, it can be argued that the effect of the respondent's SES on the respondent's aspirations would be equal to the effect of the friend's SES on the friend's aspirations; the effect of the respondent's IQ would equal the effect of the friend's IQ; the effect of the respondent's parents' aspirations would equal the corresponding effect for the friend; and the effect of the friend's SES on the respondent's aspirations would equal the effect of the respondent's SES on the friend. In terms of the coefficients, this suggests the constraints: $\gamma_{11} = \gamma_{26}$; $\gamma_{12} = \gamma_{25}$; $\gamma_{13} = \gamma_{24}$; and $\gamma_{14} = \gamma_{23}$. In model M_c in Table 3.3 these constraints have been added. The resulting model provides a significant improvement in fit, with a gain of four degrees of freedom and an increase in chi-square of 2.16 (prob = 0.75). Given the substantive motivation of the imposed constraints, it is reasonable to conclude that model M_c is the best-fitting model. //

In this example the advantage of using the software for the covariance structure model is the ability to impose equality constraints. In Example 3.2 the advantage comes from allowing the estimation of a system of equations in which some but not all of the errors in equations are correlated.

Example 3.2: estimation and hypothesis testing. Table 3.4 contains the results of estimating three models for the sociogenesis of psychological disorder. The first model, M_a (in which it is assumed that $\beta_{32} = \beta_{41} = \beta_{51} = 0$), is the model that was shown to be identified earlier in this chapter. The substantive results obtained by estimating this model are similar to those obtained by Wheaton (1978: 394-395) with a more complex covariance structure model. There is high stability in socioeconomic status, as indicated by the large and statistically significant coefficients $\hat{\beta}_{21} = 0.877$ and $\hat{\beta}_{42} = 0.844$. The respondent's father's SES has a significant effect ($\hat{\gamma}_{11} = 0.294$) on the respondent's initial SES (η_1), that diminishes for later time periods. There is also significant stability in psychological disorder as reflected in the coefficient $\hat{\beta}_{53} = 0.495$. The earliest measure of the respondent's SES (η_1) has a statistically significant effect ($\hat{\beta}_{31} = -.010$) on the earlier measure of psychological disorder (η_3). No other effects of SES on psychological disorder are significant. Note that these coefficients are *not* standardized; hence it is misleading to compare magnitudes of coefficients. For additional discussion of these results, see Wheaton (1978).

The overall fit of M_a is poor, with a chi-square of 47.9 and two degrees of freedom. Each of the parameters in the model is included for theoret-

TABLE 3.4
FIML Estimates of Three Structural Equation Models for the Sociogenesis of Psychological Disorders (Models M_a, M_b, and M_c)

	M_a		M_b		M_c	
Coefficient	*Effect*	*z*	*Effect*	*z*	*Effect*	*z*
γ_{11}	0.294	6.52	0.294	6.52	0.294	6.52
β_{21}	0.877	44.10	0.861[a]	59.11	0.896[a]	69.45
γ_{21}	0.026	1.15	0.031	1.38	0.021	0.92
β_{31}	–.010	3.80	–.010	3.90	–.010	3.72
γ_{31}	–.002	0.76	–.002	0.73	–.002	0.78
β_{42}	0.844	40.01	0.861[a]	59.11	0.896[a]	69.45
β_{43}	–.057	0.18	–.035	0.11	0.018	0.06
γ_{41}	0.060	2.50	0.055	2.33	0.046	1.93
β_{52}	–.002	0.73	–.001	0.58	–.002	0.88
β_{53}	0.495	14.95	0.495	14.96	0.495	14.92
γ_{51}	–.003	1.34	–.003	1.38	–.003	1.31
ψ_{23}	1.69	2.68	1.69	2.68	1.72	2.72
ψ_{45}	2.37	4.28	2.37	4.28	2.35	4.41
ψ_{24}	–	–	–	–	–35.31	6. 1
Chi-square	47.95		49.31		1.58	
df	2		3		2	
prob	0.000		0.000		0.454	

NOTE: Roman letters indicate that coefficients are constrained to be equal. See Figure 3.1 or text for specific meanings of coefficients. All coefficients are unstandardized and estimated by FIML (full-information maximum likelihood). Estimates were computed with LISREL V.

ical reasons and hence should not be deleted. It might be reasonable to impose an equality restriction on the coefficients relating SES at an earlier time to SES at a later time: $\beta_{21} = \beta_{42}$.[8] This restriction is imposed in the model M_b, with a resulting chi-square of 49.3 with three degrees of freedom. Since M_b is nested in M_a, the hypothesis H_0: $\beta_{21} = \beta_{42}$ can be tested with a difference of chi-square test. The result is a chi-square of 1.36 with one degree of freedom; accordingly, the hypothesis cannot be rejected at the .10 level.

Since no other restrictions seem reasonable, the addition of parameters should be considered. The maximum modification index for M_b is equal to 39.1 for ψ_{24}, suggesting a very significant improvement in fit *if the model is identified.* The resulting model, labeled M_c in Table 3.4, is identified, and freeing ψ_{24} makes substantive sense. ψ_{24} is the covariance between the equation predicting SES at time 2 (η_2) and SES at time 3 (η_4), indicating that the error in equation prdicting SES at an earlier time is correlated with the error in equation at a later time. Such correlations of error terms are called serial correlation (see Kessler and Greenberg, 1981: 87) and can indicate that variables affecting both of the dependent variables in question have been excluded from the model. For example, educational attainment can be expected to affect SES (Blau and Duncan, 1967), yet it is not included in either the equations predicting SES at time 2 or SES at time 3. The expected result of this exclusion would be the serial correlation of ζ_2 and ζ_4. Estimating M_c results in a chi-square of 1.58 with two degrees of freedom, a very acceptable fit. The interpretations of the other parameters are unchanged. //

Summary

The structural equation model presented in this chapter is important in its own right. Its presentation in the context of the covariance structure model is justified in two respects. First, those who need a structural equation model without a corresponding measurement model will find that the software developed for the covariance structure model is useful for estimating nonstandard structural equation models. Second, to apply the covariance structure model it is necessary to construct a structural equation model among the latent variables. Such a model is formally identical to the model described in this chapter, the only difference being that the variables are latent rather than observed. How the measurement model of Chapter 2 and the structural equation model of this chapter can be merged is the topic of the next chapter.

4. THE COVARIANCE STRUCTURE MODEL

The factor model estimates latent variables from observed variables without regard for the structural relations among the latent variables. Yet it is often these structural relations that are of greatest theoretical interest. The structural equation model focuses on these structural relations, but must do so by assuming that all of the variables are measured without error. The very presence of the factor model as a statistical technique indicates that this assumption may be unjustified. The covariance structure model overcomes the complementary weaknesses and combines the complementary strengths of the factor analytic and the structural equation models by merging them into a single model that simultaneously estimates latent variables from observed variables and estimates the structural relations among the latent variables. Presenting the covariance structure model turns out to be a relatively simple task since most of the work has been completed in our presentations of the confirmatory factor model and the structural equation model. All that remains to be done is to add assumptions governing the links between the two components and to indicate how our results on identification, estimation, and hypothesis testing from earlier chapters can be applied to the covariance structure model.

The Mathematical Model

The structural component of the covariance structure model consists of a structural equation model that is formally equivalent to that considered in Chapter 3:

$$\boldsymbol{\eta} = \mathbf{B}\boldsymbol{\eta} + \boldsymbol{\Gamma}\boldsymbol{\xi} + \boldsymbol{\zeta} \qquad [4.1]$$

where $\boldsymbol{\eta}$ is a (r × 1) vector of *latent*, endogenous variables; $\boldsymbol{\xi}$ is a (s × 1) vector of *latent,* exogenous variables; and $\boldsymbol{\zeta}$ is a (r × 1) vector of errors in equations. $\mathbf{B}$ is a (r × r) matrix of coefficients relating the endogenous variables to one another, and $\boldsymbol{\Gamma}$ is a (r × s) matrix of coefficients relating the exogenous variables to the endogenous variables. Equation 4.1 can be written alternatively as $\ddot{\mathbf{B}}\boldsymbol{\eta} = \boldsymbol{\Gamma}\boldsymbol{\xi} + \boldsymbol{\zeta}$, where $\ddot{\mathbf{B}}$ is defined as $(\mathbf{I} - \mathbf{B})$.

The assumptions of Chapter 3 for the structural equation model still hold. First, the variables are measured as deviations from their means: $E(\boldsymbol{\eta}) = E(\boldsymbol{\zeta}) = \mathbf{0}$ and $E(\boldsymbol{\xi}) = \mathbf{0}$. Second, there are no redundant equations: $(\mathbf{I} - \mathbf{B})^{-1} = \ddot{\mathbf{B}}^{-1}$ exists. Third, the errors in equations and the exogenous variables are uncorrelated: $E(\boldsymbol{\xi}\boldsymbol{\zeta}') = \mathbf{0}$, or equivalently, $E(\boldsymbol{\zeta}\boldsymbol{\xi}') = \mathbf{0}$. These assumptions and others related to the covariance structure model are summarized in Table 4.1.

The same definitions of covariances among variables also apply. The covariance matrix for the exogenous variables is: $\boldsymbol{\Phi} = E(\boldsymbol{\xi}\boldsymbol{\xi}')$. The covariance matrix for the errors in equations is a symmetric, not necessarily diagonal matrix: $\boldsymbol{\Psi} = E(\boldsymbol{\zeta}\boldsymbol{\zeta}')$. From Equation 4.1 and the assump-

TABLE 4.1
Summary of the Covariance Structure Model

Matrix	*Dimension*	*Mean*	*Covariance*	*Dimension*	*Description*
$\boldsymbol{\eta}$	$(r \times 1)$	**0**	$COV(\boldsymbol{\eta}) = E(\boldsymbol{\eta\eta}')$	$(r \times r)$	latent endogenous variables
$\boldsymbol{\xi}$	$(s \times 1)$	**0**	$\boldsymbol{\Phi} = E(\boldsymbol{\xi\xi}')$	$(s \times s)$	latent exogenous variables
$\boldsymbol{\zeta}$	$(r \times 1)$	**0**	$\boldsymbol{\Psi} = E(\boldsymbol{\zeta\zeta}')$	$(r \times r)$	errors in equations
$\mathbf{B}$	$(r \times r)$	—	—	—	direct effects of $\boldsymbol{\eta}$ on $\boldsymbol{\eta}$
$\ddot{\mathbf{B}}$	$(r \times r)$	—	—	—	defined as $(\mathbf{I} - \mathbf{B})$
$\boldsymbol{\Gamma}$	$(r \times s)$	—	—	—	direct effects of $\boldsymbol{\xi}$ on $\boldsymbol{\eta}$
$\mathbf{x}$	$(q \times 1)$	**0**	$\boldsymbol{\Sigma}_{xx} = E(\mathbf{xx}')$	$(q \times q)$	observed exogenous variables
$\boldsymbol{\Lambda}_x$	$(q \times s)$	—	—	—	loadings of $\mathbf{x}$ on $\boldsymbol{\xi}$
$\boldsymbol{\delta}$	$(q \times 1)$	**0**	$\boldsymbol{\Theta}_\delta = E(\boldsymbol{\delta\delta}')$	$(q \times q)$	unique factors for $\mathbf{x}$
$\mathbf{y}$	$(p \times 1)$	**0**	$\boldsymbol{\Sigma}_{yy} = E(\mathbf{yy}')$	$(p \times p)$	observed endogenous variables
$\boldsymbol{\Lambda}_y$	$(p \times r)$	—	—	—	loadings of $\mathbf{y}$ on $\boldsymbol{\eta}$
$\boldsymbol{\epsilon}$	$(p \times 1)$	**0**	$\boldsymbol{\Theta}_\epsilon = E(\boldsymbol{\epsilon\epsilon}')$	$(p \times p)$	unique factors for $\mathbf{y}$

Structural Equations:

$$\boldsymbol{\eta} = \mathbf{B}\boldsymbol{\eta} + \boldsymbol{\Gamma\xi} + \boldsymbol{\zeta} \quad [4.1]$$

$$\ddot{\mathbf{B}}\boldsymbol{\eta} = \boldsymbol{\Gamma\xi} + \boldsymbol{\zeta}$$

Factor Equations:

$$\mathbf{x} = \boldsymbol{\Lambda}_x\boldsymbol{\xi} + \boldsymbol{\delta} \quad [4.2]$$

$$\mathbf{y} = \boldsymbol{\Lambda}_y\boldsymbol{\eta} + \boldsymbol{\epsilon} \quad [4.3]$$

Covariance Equation:

$$\boldsymbol{\Sigma} = \left[\begin{array}{c|c} \boldsymbol{\Lambda}_y\ddot{\mathbf{B}}^{-1}(\boldsymbol{\Gamma\Phi\Gamma}' + \boldsymbol{\Psi})\ddot{\mathbf{B}}'^{-1}\boldsymbol{\Lambda}_y' + \boldsymbol{\Theta}_\epsilon & \boldsymbol{\Lambda}_y\ddot{\mathbf{B}}^{-1}\boldsymbol{\Gamma\Phi\Lambda}_x' \\ \hline \boldsymbol{\Lambda}_x\boldsymbol{\Phi\Gamma}'\ddot{\mathbf{B}}'^{-1}\boldsymbol{\Lambda}_y' & \boldsymbol{\Lambda}_x\boldsymbol{\Phi\Lambda}_x' + \boldsymbol{\Theta}_\delta \end{array}\right] \quad [4.4]$$

Assumptions:

a. Variables are measured from their means: $E(\boldsymbol{\eta}) = E(\boldsymbol{\zeta}) = \mathbf{0}$; $E(\boldsymbol{\xi}) = \mathbf{0}$; $E(\mathbf{x}) = E(\boldsymbol{\delta}) = \mathbf{0}$; $E(\mathbf{y}) = E(\boldsymbol{\epsilon}) = \mathbf{0}$.

b. Common and unique factors are uncorrelated: $E(\boldsymbol{\xi\delta}') = \mathbf{0}$ or $E(\boldsymbol{\delta\xi}') = \mathbf{0}$; $E(\boldsymbol{\eta\epsilon}') = \mathbf{0}$ or $E(\boldsymbol{\epsilon\eta}') = \mathbf{0}$; $E(\boldsymbol{\xi\epsilon}') = \mathbf{0}$ or $E(\boldsymbol{\epsilon\xi}') = \mathbf{0}$; $E(\boldsymbol{\eta\delta}') = \mathbf{0}$ or $E(\boldsymbol{\delta\eta}') = \mathbf{0}$.

c. Unique factors and errors in equations are uncorrelated across equations: $E(\boldsymbol{\delta\epsilon}') = \mathbf{0}$ or $E(\boldsymbol{\epsilon\delta}') = \mathbf{0}$; $E(\boldsymbol{\zeta\delta}') = \mathbf{0}$ or $E(\boldsymbol{\delta\zeta}') = \mathbf{0}$; $E(\boldsymbol{\zeta\epsilon}') = \mathbf{0}$ or $E(\boldsymbol{\epsilon\zeta}') = \mathbf{0}$.

d. Exogenous variables and errors in equations are uncorrelated: $E(\boldsymbol{\xi\zeta}') = \mathbf{0}$ or $E(\boldsymbol{\zeta\xi}') = \mathbf{0}$.

e. None of the structural equations is redundant: $\ddot{\mathbf{B}}^{-1} = (\mathbf{I} - \mathbf{B})^{-1}$ exits.

tions of the model, the covariance matrix for the endogenous variables is $COV(\boldsymbol{\eta}) = E(\boldsymbol{\eta\eta}') = \ddot{\mathbf{B}}^{-1}(\boldsymbol{\Gamma\Phi\Gamma}' + \boldsymbol{\Psi})\ddot{\mathbf{B}}'^{-1}$ (as derived in Chapter 3).

Unlike the structural equation model considered in Chapter 3, $\boldsymbol{\eta}$ and $\boldsymbol{\xi}$ are not required to be observed variables, although some of them may be observed. Rather, $\boldsymbol{\eta}$ and $\boldsymbol{\xi}$ are related to the observed variables **x** and **y** by a pair of confirmatory factor models:

$$\mathbf{x} = \boldsymbol{\Lambda}_x\boldsymbol{\xi} + \boldsymbol{\delta} \qquad [4.2]$$

$$\mathbf{y} = \boldsymbol{\Lambda}_y\boldsymbol{\eta} + \boldsymbol{\epsilon} \qquad [4.3]$$

where **x** is a $(q \times 1)$ vector of *observed* exogenous variables and **y** is a $(p \times 1)$ vector of *observed* endogenous variables. $\boldsymbol{\Lambda}_x$ is a $(q \times s)$ matrix of loadings of the observed x-variables on the latent ξ-variables, and $\boldsymbol{\Lambda}_y$ is a $(p \times r)$ matrix of loadings of the observed y-variables on the latent η-variables. $\boldsymbol{\delta}$ of dimension $(q \times 1)$ and $\boldsymbol{\epsilon}$ of dimension $(p \times 1)$ are vectors of unique factors. Within each factor model, the unique factors may be correlated. That is, $COV(\boldsymbol{\delta}) = E(\boldsymbol{\delta\delta}') = \boldsymbol{\Theta}_\delta$ and $COV(\boldsymbol{\epsilon}) = E(\boldsymbol{\epsilon\epsilon}') = \boldsymbol{\Theta}_\epsilon$ are symmetric, but not necessarily diagonal. Note that equations 4.2 and 4.3 are identical to equations 2.1 and 2.2.

As with the factor models of Chapter 2, common factors are assumed to be uncorrelated with unique factors, both within equations—$E(\boldsymbol{\xi\delta}') = \mathbf{0}$ or $E(\boldsymbol{\delta\xi}') = \mathbf{0}$, and $E(\boldsymbol{\eta\epsilon}') = \mathbf{0}$ or $E(\boldsymbol{\epsilon\eta}') = \mathbf{0}$—and across equations—$E(\boldsymbol{\xi\epsilon}') = \mathbf{0}$ or $E(\boldsymbol{\epsilon\xi}') = \mathbf{0}$, and $E(\boldsymbol{\eta\delta}') = \mathbf{0}$ or $E(\boldsymbol{\delta\eta}') = \mathbf{0}$. Finally, it is assumed that the δ's, ϵ's, and ζ's are mutually uncorrelated: $E(\boldsymbol{\delta\epsilon}') = \mathbf{0}$ or $E(\boldsymbol{\epsilon\delta}') = \mathbf{0}$; $E(\boldsymbol{\delta\zeta}') = \mathbf{0}$ or $E(\boldsymbol{\zeta\delta}') = \mathbf{0}$; and $E(\boldsymbol{\epsilon\zeta}') = \mathbf{0}$ or $E(\boldsymbol{\zeta\epsilon}') = \mathbf{0}$.

The Covariance Structure

Since the variables are measured as deviations from their means, the covariance matrix for the observed variables can be defined as

$$\boldsymbol{\Sigma} = E\left[\begin{bmatrix}\mathbf{y}\\ \hline \mathbf{x}\end{bmatrix}\begin{bmatrix}\mathbf{y}\\ \hline \mathbf{x}\end{bmatrix}'\right] = E\left[\begin{array}{c|c}\mathbf{yy}' & \mathbf{yx}'\\ \hline \mathbf{xy}' & \mathbf{xx}'\end{array}\right]$$

where $\begin{bmatrix}\mathbf{y}\\ \hline \mathbf{x}\end{bmatrix}$ is the $(p+q \times 1)$ vector formed by stacking **y** on top of **x**. Substituting equations 4.2 and 4.3 for **x** and **y** results in

$$\boldsymbol{\Sigma} = E\left[\begin{array}{c|c}(\boldsymbol{\Lambda}_y\boldsymbol{\eta} + \boldsymbol{\epsilon})(\boldsymbol{\Lambda}_y\boldsymbol{\eta} + \boldsymbol{\epsilon})' & (\boldsymbol{\Lambda}_y\boldsymbol{\eta} + \boldsymbol{\epsilon})(\boldsymbol{\Lambda}_x\boldsymbol{\xi} + \boldsymbol{\delta})'\\ \hline (\boldsymbol{\Lambda}_x\boldsymbol{\xi} + \boldsymbol{\delta})(\boldsymbol{\Lambda}_y\boldsymbol{\eta} + \boldsymbol{\epsilon})' & (\boldsymbol{\Lambda}_x\boldsymbol{\xi} + \boldsymbol{\delta})(\boldsymbol{\Lambda}_x\boldsymbol{\xi} + \boldsymbol{\delta})'\end{array}\right]$$

Upon multiplying,

$$\Sigma = E\left[\begin{array}{c|c} \Lambda_y\eta\eta'\Lambda_y' + \epsilon\epsilon' & \Lambda_y\eta\xi'\Lambda_x' + \epsilon\delta' \\ + \Lambda_y\eta\epsilon' + \epsilon\eta'\Lambda_y' & + \Lambda_y\eta\delta' + \epsilon\xi'\Lambda_x' \\ \hline \Lambda_x\xi\eta'\Lambda_y' + \delta\epsilon' & \Lambda_x\xi\xi'\Lambda_x' + \delta\delta' \\ + \Lambda_x\xi\epsilon' + \delta\eta'\Lambda_y' & + \Lambda_x\xi\delta' + \delta\xi'\Lambda_x' \end{array}\right]$$

By distributing the expectation operator, making use of the assumed zero covariances among the variables, and applying the definitions of the covariances among variables, the desired result is obtained:

$$\Sigma = \left[\begin{array}{c|c} \Lambda_y\ddot{B}^{-1}(\Gamma\Phi\Gamma' + \Psi)\ddot{B}'^{-1}\Lambda_y' + \Theta_\epsilon & \Lambda_y\ddot{B}^{-1}\Gamma\Phi\Lambda_x' \\ \hline \Lambda_x\Phi\Gamma'\ddot{B}'^{-1}\Lambda_y' & \Lambda_x\Phi\Lambda_x' + \Theta_\delta \end{array}\right] \qquad [4.4]$$

This rather imposing equation relates the variances and covariances of the observed variables to the parameters of the model. Assuming that the model is identified, estimation involves finding values for the eight parameter matrices that produce an estimate of $\mathbf{\Sigma}$ according to equation 4.4 that is as close as possible to the sample matrix **S**.

Special Cases of the Covariance Structure Model

Before discussing estimation and the preliminary issue of identification, it is informative to consider the confirmatory factor model and the structural equation model as special cases of the covariance structure model. Considering these models as special cases is not only useful for understanding the general model, it is also useful for understanding how software for the covariance structure model can be used to estimate other types of models.

The factor analytic model. Assume that $\mathbf{B} = \mathbf{I}$ (or $\ddot{\mathbf{B}} = \mathbf{0}$), $\mathbf{\Gamma} = \mathbf{0}$, $\mathbf{\Psi} = \mathbf{0}$, $\mathbf{\Lambda}_y = \mathbf{0}$, and $\mathbf{\Theta}_\epsilon = \mathbf{0}$. These constraints reduce the structural component of the covariance structure model to $\boldsymbol{\zeta} = \mathbf{0}$, with the ζ's having variances of zero. The measurement model for the y-variables is reduced to $\mathbf{y} = \boldsymbol{\epsilon}$, where the ϵ's must equal zero (since $E(\boldsymbol{\epsilon}) = \mathbf{0}$ and $COV(\boldsymbol{\epsilon}) = \mathbf{0}$). The measurement equation for the x's is identical to equation 2.1: $\mathbf{x} = \mathbf{\Lambda}_x\boldsymbol{\xi} + \boldsymbol{\delta}$. When the constraints are applied to the covariance equation 4.4, it reduces to $\mathbf{\Sigma} = \mathbf{\Lambda}_x\mathbf{\Phi}\mathbf{\Lambda}_x' + \mathbf{\Theta}_\delta$, which is identical to the upper-left partition of equation 2.3.

Similarly, a factor model among the y-variables is obtained by restricting $\mathbf{B} = \mathbf{0}$ (or $\ddot{\mathbf{B}} = \mathbf{I}$), $\mathbf{\Gamma} = \mathbf{0}$, $\mathbf{\Lambda}_x = \mathbf{0}$, and $\mathbf{\Theta}_\epsilon = \mathbf{0}$. These constraints eliminate the measurement model for the x's. The structural equation is reduced to $\boldsymbol{\eta} = \boldsymbol{\zeta}$, with $\mathrm{COV}(\boldsymbol{\eta}) = \mathbf{\Psi}$. Thus, $\mathbf{\Psi}$ is equivalent to $\mathbf{\Phi}$ in the factor model for the x's. When the imposed constraints are applied to equation 4.4, the resulting covariance equation is $\mathbf{\Sigma} = \mathbf{\Lambda}_y\mathbf{\Psi}\mathbf{\Lambda}_y' + \mathbf{\Theta}_\epsilon$.

Structural equation model. The measurement model can be eliminated from the covariance structure model by equating the observed variables to the latent variables. This is accomplished by constraining the parameters $\mathbf{\Lambda}_x = \mathbf{I}$, $\mathbf{\Theta}_\delta = \mathbf{0}$, $\mathbf{\Lambda}_y = \mathbf{I}$, $\mathbf{\Theta}_\epsilon = \mathbf{0}$. Equations 4.2 and 4.3 are reduced to $\mathbf{x} = \boldsymbol{\xi}$ and $\mathbf{y} = \boldsymbol{\eta}$, indicating that the latent variables are exactly equal to the observed variables. Equation 4.1, which is equivalent to equation 3.1, is left unchanged. The covariance equation for the structural equation model (equation 3.5) is obtained from equation 4.4 by imposing the constraints $\mathbf{\Lambda}_x = \mathbf{I}$, $\mathbf{\Theta}_\delta = \mathbf{0}$, $\mathbf{\Lambda}_y = \mathbf{I}$, and $\mathbf{\Theta}_\epsilon = \mathbf{0}$. The special cases of the structural equation model considered in Chapter 3 can be obtained by imposing constraints on $\mathbf{B}$, $\mathbf{\Gamma}$, and $\mathbf{\Psi}$. Thus, the structural equation model is a special case of the covariance structure model, and can be estimated with software for the covariance structure model if the necessary constraints are imposed. (These special cases are not discussed further in this chapter.)

Examples

To illustrate specification, identification, estimation, and hypothesis testing, two examples that contain both measurement and structural components are used.

Example 4.1: a panel model with measurement error. This example combines the measurement model in Example 1 of *CFA* with the panel model in Example 3.2. It is roughly equivalent to the model analyzed by Wheaton (1978), although a number of changes have been made to simplify the presentation. Figure 4.1 diagrams the basic model.

There is one exogenous variable measuring father's SES (ξ_1), and endogenous variables corresponding to the respondent's SES at three points in time (η_1, η_2, and η_4) and the respondent's psychological dis-

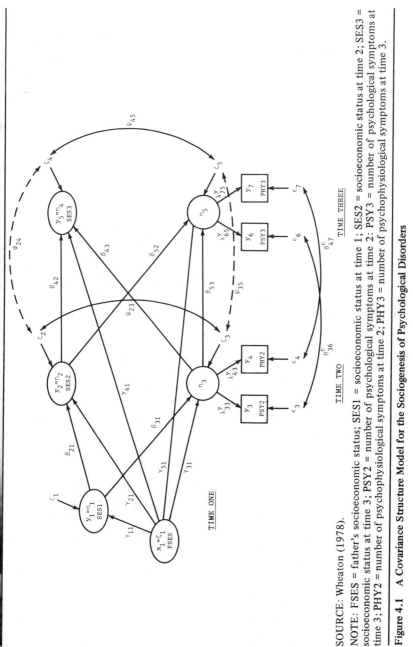

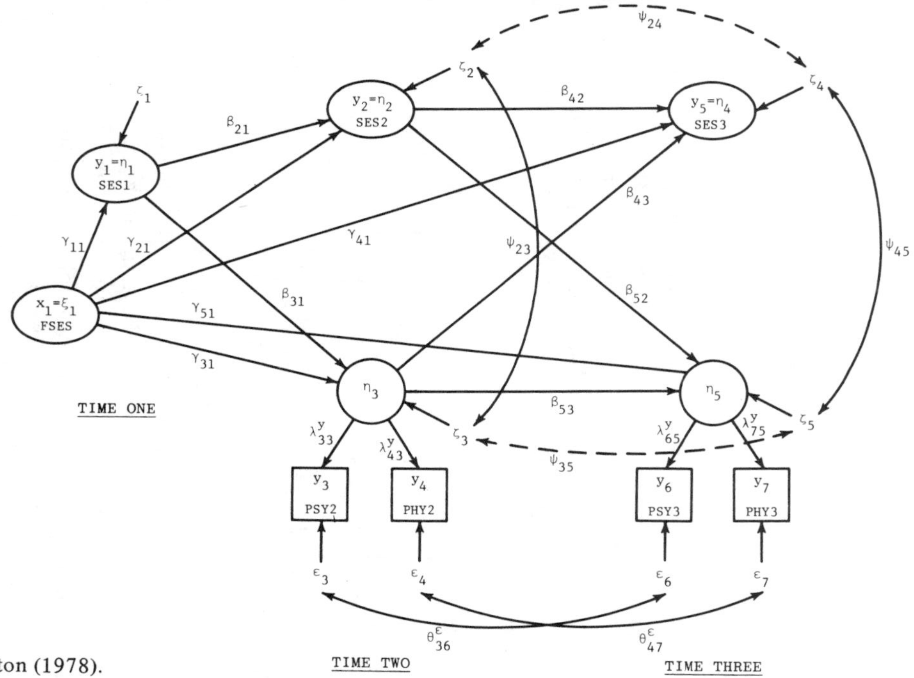

SOURCE: Wheaton (1978).

NOTE: FSES = father's socioeconomic status; SES1 = socioeconomic status at time 1; SES2 = socioeconomic status at time 2; SES3 = socioeconomic status at time 3; PSY2 = number of psychological symptoms at time 2: PSY3 = number of psychological symptoms at time 3; PHY2 = number of psychophysiological symptoms at time 2; PHY3 = number of psychophysiological symptoms at time 3.

Figure 4.1 A Covariance Structure Model for the Sociogenesis of Psychological Disorders

order at two points in time (η_3 and η_5). The structural model is identical to the final, identified version of Example 3.2:

$$\begin{bmatrix} \eta_1 \\ \eta_2 \\ \eta_3 \\ \eta_4 \\ \eta_5 \end{bmatrix} = \begin{bmatrix} \underline{0} & \underline{0} & \underline{0} & \underline{0} & \underline{0} \\ \beta_{21} & \underline{0} & \underline{0} & \underline{0} & \underline{0} \\ \beta_{31} & \underline{0} & \underline{0} & \underline{0} & \underline{0} \\ \underline{0} & \beta_{42} & \beta_{43} & \underline{0} & \underline{0} \\ \underline{0} & \beta_{52} & \beta_{53} & \underline{0} & \underline{0} \end{bmatrix} \begin{bmatrix} \eta_1 \\ \eta_2 \\ \eta_3 \\ \eta_4 \\ \eta_5 \end{bmatrix} + \begin{bmatrix} \gamma_{11} \\ \gamma_{21} \\ \gamma_{31} \\ \gamma_{41} \\ \gamma_{51} \end{bmatrix} \begin{bmatrix} \xi_1 \end{bmatrix} + \begin{bmatrix} \zeta_1 \\ \zeta_2 \\ \zeta_3 \\ \zeta_4 \\ \zeta_5 \end{bmatrix}$$

Initially it is assumed that errors in equations are uncorrelated, except for errors predicting variables at the same time. Thus, the errors in the equations predicting SES at time two and psychological disorder at time two are correlated, and the errors in the equations predicting SES at time three and psychological disorder at time three are correlated. The resulting $\mathbf{\Psi}$ is

$$\mathbf{\Psi} = \begin{bmatrix} \psi_{11} & \underline{0} & \underline{0} & \underline{0} & \underline{0} \\ \underline{0} & \psi_{22} & \psi_{23} & \underline{0} & \underline{0} \\ \underline{0} & \psi_{32} & \psi_{33} & \underline{0} & \underline{0} \\ \underline{0} & \underline{0} & \underline{0} & \psi_{44} & \psi_{45} \\ \underline{0} & \underline{0} & \underline{0} & \psi_{54} & \psi_{55} \end{bmatrix}$$

Unlike Example 3.2, a measurement model is used to link the observed variables to latent variables. Father's SES (ξ_1) is assumed to be measured without error, so that $x_1 = \xi_1$. In terms of the measurement equation 4.2, $\mathbf{\Lambda}_x$ is restricted to $\mathbf{I}$, and $\mathbf{\Theta}_\delta$ is restricted to $\mathbf{0}$: $\mathbf{x} = \mathbf{I}\boldsymbol{\xi} + \mathbf{0}$, or $\mathbf{x} = \boldsymbol{\xi}$. The measurement model for the y-variables is more complicated. The latent variables for the respondent's SES (η_1, η_2, and η_4) are assumed to be measured without error by y_1, y_2, and y_5. This involves the restrictions $\lambda^y_{11} = \lambda^y_{22} = \lambda^y_{54} = 1$ and $\theta^\epsilon_{11} = \theta^\epsilon_{22} = \theta^\epsilon_{55} = 0$. Each latent variable for psychological disorder is measured by two observed variables: the number of psychological symptoms and the number of psychophysiological symptoms. Thus, y_3 and y_4 load on η_3 with loadings λ^y_{33} and λ^y_{43}, and y_6 and y_7 load on η_5 with loadings λ^y_{65} and λ^y_{75}. The loadings λ^y_{33} and λ^y_{65} are fixed to one to set the metrics of η_3 and η_5, respectively (see Chapter 2 of *CFA*). Since COV($\boldsymbol{\eta}$) is not a fundamental parameter (i.e., it is defined in terms of other parameter matrices), the metric of the η-variables can be set only by restricting the loadings in $\mathbf{\Lambda}_y$. The resulting measurement equation for the y's is

$$\begin{bmatrix} y_1 \\ y_2 \\ y_3 \\ y_4 \\ y_5 \\ y_6 \\ y_7 \end{bmatrix} = \begin{bmatrix} \underline{1} & \underline{0} & \underline{0} & \underline{0} & \underline{0} \\ \underline{0} & \underline{1} & \underline{0} & \underline{0} & \underline{0} \\ \underline{0} & \underline{0} & \underline{1} & \underline{0} & \underline{0} \\ \underline{0} & \underline{0} & \lambda_{43}^{y} & \underline{0} & \underline{0} \\ \underline{0} & \underline{0} & \underline{0} & \underline{1} & \underline{0} \\ \underline{0} & \underline{0} & \underline{0} & \underline{0} & \underline{1} \\ \underline{0} & \underline{0} & \underline{0} & \underline{0} & \lambda_{75}^{y} \end{bmatrix} \begin{bmatrix} \eta_1 \\ \eta_2 \\ \eta_3 \\ \eta_4 \\ \eta_5 \end{bmatrix} + \begin{bmatrix} \underline{0} \\ \underline{0} \\ \epsilon_3 \\ \epsilon_4 \\ \underline{0} \\ \epsilon_6 \\ \epsilon_7 \end{bmatrix}$$

As was the case with Example 1 of *CFA*, it is assumed that errors in measurement for the same variables measured at different times are correlated. That is, $\theta_{36}^{\epsilon} \neq 0$ and $\theta_{47}^{\epsilon} \neq 0$. Since y_1, y_2, and y_5 are assumed to be measured without error, $\theta_{11}^{\epsilon} = \theta_{22}^{\epsilon} = \theta_{55}^{\epsilon} = 0$. The resulting covariance matrix is

$$\mathbf{\Theta}_{\epsilon} = \begin{bmatrix} \underline{0} & \underline{0} & \underline{0} & \underline{0} & \underline{0} & \underline{0} & \underline{0} \\ \underline{0} & \underline{0} & \underline{0} & \underline{0} & \underline{0} & \underline{0} & \underline{0} \\ \underline{0} & \underline{0} & \theta_{33}^{\epsilon} & \underline{0} & \underline{0} & \theta_{36}^{\epsilon} & \underline{0} \\ \underline{0} & \underline{0} & \underline{0} & \theta_{44}^{\epsilon} & \underline{0} & \underline{0} & \theta_{47}^{\epsilon} \\ \underline{0} & \underline{0} & \underline{0} & \underline{0} & \underline{0} & \underline{0} & \underline{0} \\ \underline{0} & \underline{0} & \theta_{63}^{\epsilon} & \underline{0} & \underline{0} & \theta_{66}^{\epsilon} & \underline{0} \\ \underline{0} & \underline{0} & \underline{0} & \theta_{74}^{\epsilon} & \underline{0} & \underline{0} & \theta_{77}^{\epsilon} \end{bmatrix}$$

The measurement model is represented in Figure 4.1 in two ways. When no measurement error is present, an observed and latent variable are both contained in the same oval. When measurement error is present, an observed variable is contained in a square linked by an arrow to a latent variable contained in a circle. //

Example 4.2: a nonrecursive model with measurement error. Our second example extends Example 3.3 by adding a measurement model for the endogenous variables, leaving the structural model unchanged. This model is diagrammed in Figure 4.2.

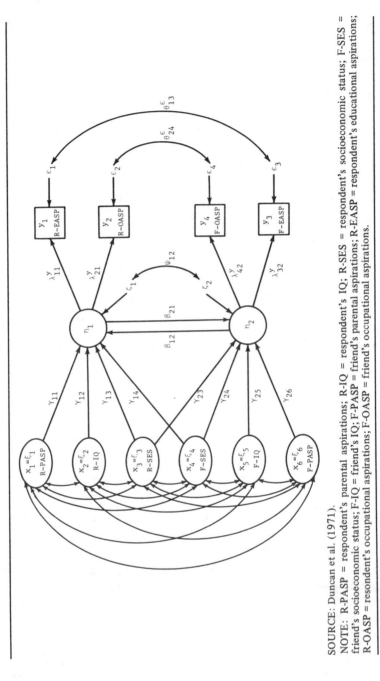

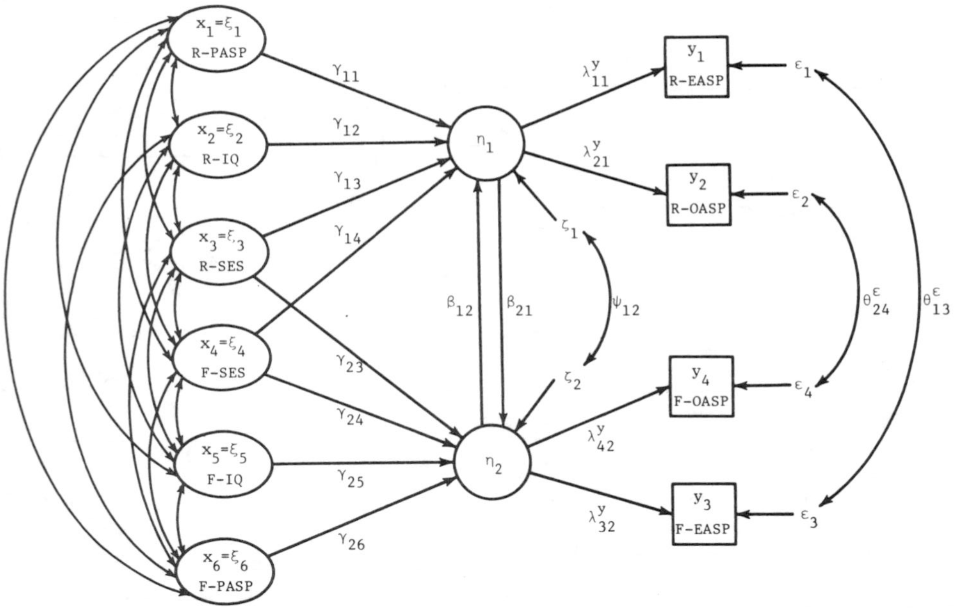

SOURCE: Duncan et al. (1971).

NOTE: R-PASP = respondent's parental aspirations; R-IQ = respondent's IQ; R-SES = respondent's socioeconomic status; F-SES = friend's socioeconomic status; F-IQ = friend's IQ; F-PASP = friend's parental aspirations; R-EASP = respondent's educational aspirations; R-OASP = resondent's occupational aspirations; F-OASP = friend's occupational aspirations.

Figure 4.2 A Covariance Structure Model of Peer Influences on Aspirations

The exogenous variables are assumed to be measured without error. That is, $\mathbf{x} = \boldsymbol{\xi}$, with the constraints $\boldsymbol{\Lambda}_x = \mathbf{I}$ and $\boldsymbol{\Theta}_\delta = \mathbf{0}$. Each of the endogenous variables has two indicators. η_1, the common factor for respondent's ambitions, is measured with y_1, the respondent's educational aspirations, and y_2, the respondent's occupational aspirations. Similarly, η_2, the common factor for the friend's ambition, is measured by y_3 and y_4. The measurement model for the η's is

$$\begin{bmatrix} y_1 \\ y_2 \\ y_3 \\ y_4 \end{bmatrix} = \begin{bmatrix} \underline{1} & \underline{0} \\ \lambda^y_{21} & \underline{0} \\ \underline{0} & \underline{1} \\ \underline{0} & \lambda^y_{42} \end{bmatrix} \begin{bmatrix} \eta_1 \\ \eta_2 \end{bmatrix} + \begin{bmatrix} \epsilon_1 \\ \epsilon_2 \\ \epsilon_3 \\ \epsilon_4 \end{bmatrix}$$

where λ^y_{11} and λ^y_{32} have been fixed to one to establish the metric of η_1 and η_2. Duncan et al. (1971) assumed that the measurement errors were correlated as indicated by the matrix

$$\boldsymbol{\Theta}_\epsilon = \begin{bmatrix} \theta^\epsilon_{11} & \underline{0} & \theta^\epsilon_{13} & \theta^\epsilon_{14} \\ \underline{0} & \theta^\epsilon_{22} & \theta^\epsilon_{23} & \theta^\epsilon_{24} \\ \theta^\epsilon_{31} & \theta^\epsilon_{32} & \theta^\epsilon_{33} & \underline{0} \\ \theta^\epsilon_{41} & \theta^\epsilon_{42} & \underline{0} & \theta^\epsilon_{44} \end{bmatrix}$$

θ^ϵ_{13} and θ^ϵ_{24} (and accordingly, θ^ϵ_{31} and θ^ϵ_{42}) indicate that the errors in the measurement of the respondent's and the friend's occupational aspirations are correlated, as are the errors in the measurement of the respondent's and friend's educational aspirations. Since similar errors in measuring occupational aspirations may have been made with both a respondent and his friend, these correlations are reasonable. θ^ϵ_{14} $(= \theta^\epsilon_{41})$ and θ^ϵ_{23} $(= \theta^\epsilon_{32})$ indicate that measures of friend's educational aspirations and respondent's occupational aspirations (and vice versa) are correlated. This seems unnecessary. If errors in the measurement of educational and occupational aspirations were correlated, it would be more reasonable to assume they were correlated in measures for the same person (i.e., θ^ϵ_{12} and θ^ϵ_{34}). Accordingly, θ^ϵ_{23} and θ^ϵ_{14} are constrained to zero in our analysis. //

Identification

As with the factor analytic and the structural equation models, identification must be demonstrated before estimation can proceed. Identification in the covariance structure model adds no new complications to our previous discussions. Difficulty is increased only because of the greater number of parameters that are often contained in covariance structure models.

A necessary condition for identification is that the number of independent parameters being estimated is less than or equal to the number of nonredundant elements of **S**, the sample matrix of covariances among observed variables. In counting the number of independent parameters, the symmetry of covariance matrices and imposed equality constraints must be taken into account. Thus, for example, if $\gamma_{11} = \gamma_{12} = \gamma_{13} = \gamma_{14}$ is an imposed constraint, the four parameters include only one independent parameter, since once the value of one parameter is known, the values of the others are also known. If, for example, ψ_{12} is a free parameter (since $\psi_{12} = \psi_{21}$ due to the symmetry of $\mathbf{\Psi}$) ψ_{12} and ψ_{21} make up only one independent parameter. If t is the number of independent parameters in a covariance structure model, the necessary condition for identification is $t \leq \frac{1}{2}(p + q)(p + q + 1)$.

Unfortunately, no easily applicable sufficient, or necessary and sufficient, conditions for the full covariance structure model are available, although the conditions for the special cases considered earlier apply as appropriate. In general, identification must be proven by solving for the parameters of the model in terms of the variances and covariances of the observed variables. This is most easily achieved by first demonstrating that the parameters of the measurement model are identified, including the variances and covariances of the factors. Once covariances among the factors are known to be identified, the structural parameters can be identified by solving for them in terms of the covariances among the factors, rather than trying to solve them directly in terms of the covariances among the observed variables. This is sufficient for identification since, in identifying the measurement model, it was proven that the covariances among the factors could be solved for in terms of the covariances among the observed variables. Note that solving the structural parameters in terms of the variances and covariances among the factors is not sufficient for identification unless the variances and covariances among the factors have first been solved for in terms of the variances and covariances among the observed variables.

Proving that a model is identified can be quite difficult. Jöreskog and Sörbom (1978) argued that the computer can be used to determine if a model is identified. In computing maximum likelihood estimates of parameters, the information matrix is computed. (See Kmenta [1971: 174-186] for a discussion of the information matrix.) Roughly speaking, the information matrix corresponds to a matrix of variances and covariances of the parameter estimates. Jöreskog and Sörbom (1978: 11) stated

> If [the information matrix] is positive definite it is *almost certain* that the model is identified. On the other hand, if the information matrix is singular, the model is not identified [italics added].

The reader is warned that this is not a sufficient condition for identification. If the information matrix is positive definite, it is possible (even if unlikely) that the model is not identified and that the estimates of the parameters are arbitrary and meaningless. On the other hand, if identification has been "proven" by solving the parameters in terms of the variances and covariances of the observed variables, and the program indicates that the information matrix is *not* positive definite, an error in proving identification or in running the program may have been made. If the positive definiteness of the information matrix is used to "prove" that a model is identified (which is *not* recommended), a procedure suggested by Jöreskog (1978) should be implemented. If a model appears to be identified according to the information matrix, try several different sets of starting values as input to the maximum likelihood estimation program. If the resulting estimates are all equal, one can be more confident, albeit still uncertain, that the model is identified. Still, if one happens to estimate a model where the "almost certain" condition is satisfied, but the model is not identified, the resulting analyses are meaningless. The emphatic recommendation is: always prove that a model is identified by solving the model's parameters in terms of the variances and covariances of the observed variables.

Example 4.1: identification. The structural equations in this example are identical to those in Example 3.2 (compare Figures 3.1 and 4.1). The only difference is that the variables in the structural model in Example 3.2 are observed, whereas in this example some of them are latent. In Example 3.2 identification was proven by showing that each of the β's, γ's, and ψ's could be solved for in terms of the variances and covariances of the observed η's and ξ's. Since the structural equations are identical in this example, the same algebraic manipulations can be used to solve for each of the parameters in terms of the variances and covariances of the latent variables. If the variances and covariances for the latent variables are identified, then the structural component of this example is identified.

To identify the variances and covariances of the latent variables it must be shown that each can be solved for in terms of the variances and covariances of the observed variables. Since it is the measurement model that links the observed variables to the latent variables, we must begin with the measurement equations. These are

$$x_1 = \xi_1 \qquad y_1 = \eta_1 \qquad y_2 = \eta_2$$

$$y_3 = \eta_3 + \epsilon_3 \qquad y_4 = \lambda^y_{43}\eta_3 + \epsilon_4 \qquad y_5 = \eta_4$$

$$y_6 = \eta_5 + \epsilon_6 \qquad y_7 = \lambda^y_{75}\eta_5 + \epsilon_7$$

The covariances among the x's and y's can be computed by multiplying each pair of measurement equations, taking expectations, and making use of the assumptions that certain variables are uncorrelated. (To clearly indicate where covariances have been assumed to equal zero, such covariances are written with a line crossing them out.) The variances of the observed variables are

$$\sigma_{x1x1} = \phi_{11}$$
$$\sigma_{y1y1} = \mathrm{VAR}(\eta_1)$$
$$\sigma_{y2y2} = \mathrm{VAR}(\eta_2)$$
$$\sigma_{y3y3} = \mathrm{VAR}(\eta_3) + \theta^\epsilon_{33} + 2\cancel{\mathrm{COV}(\eta_3,\epsilon_3)}$$
$$\sigma_{y4y4} = \lambda^{y\,2}_{43}\,\mathrm{VAR}(\eta_3) + \theta^\epsilon_{44} + 2\lambda^y_{43}\,\cancel{\mathrm{COV}(\eta_3,\epsilon_4)}$$
$$\sigma_{y5y5} = \mathrm{VAR}(\eta_4)$$
$$\sigma_{y6y6} = \mathrm{VAR}(\eta_5) + \theta^\epsilon_{66} + 2\cancel{\mathrm{COV}(\eta_5,\epsilon_6)}$$
$$\sigma_{y7y7} = \lambda^{y\,2}_{75}\,\mathrm{VAR}(\eta_5) + \theta^\epsilon_{77} + 2\lambda^y_{75}\,\cancel{\mathrm{COV}(\eta_5,\epsilon_7)}$$

The covariances among the observed variables are

$$\sigma_{x1y1} = \mathrm{COV}(\xi_1,\eta_1)$$
$$\sigma_{x1y2} = \mathrm{COV}(\xi_1,\eta_2)$$
$$\sigma_{x1y3} = \mathrm{COV}(\xi_1,\eta_3) + \cancel{\mathrm{COV}(\xi_1,\epsilon_3)}$$

$$\sigma_{x1y4} = \lambda^y_{43}\,\mathrm{COV}(\xi_1,\eta_3) + \cancel{\mathrm{COV}(\xi_1,\epsilon_4)}$$

$$\sigma_{x1y5} = \mathrm{COV}(\xi_1,\eta_4)$$

$$\sigma_{x1y6} = \mathrm{COV}(\xi_1,\eta_5) + \cancel{\mathrm{COV}(\xi_1,\epsilon_6)}$$

$$\sigma_{x1y7} = \lambda^y_{75}\,\mathrm{COV}(\xi_1,\eta_5) + \cancel{\mathrm{COV}(\xi_1,\epsilon_7)}$$

$$\sigma_{y1y2} = \mathrm{COV}(\eta_1,\eta_2)$$

$$\sigma_{y1y3} = \mathrm{COV}(\eta_1,\eta_3) + \cancel{\mathrm{COV}(\eta_1,\epsilon_3)}$$

$$\sigma_{y1y4} = \lambda^y_{43}\,\mathrm{COV}(\eta_1,\eta_3) + \cancel{\mathrm{COV}(\eta_1,\epsilon_4)}$$

$$\sigma_{y1y5} = \mathrm{COV}(\eta_1,\eta_4)$$

$$\sigma_{y1y6} = \mathrm{COV}(\eta_1,\eta_5) + \cancel{\mathrm{COV}(\eta_1,\epsilon_6)}$$

$$\sigma_{y1y7} = \lambda^y_{75}\,\mathrm{COV}(\eta_1,\eta_5) + \cancel{\mathrm{COV}(\eta_1,\epsilon_7)}$$

$$\sigma_{y2y3} = \mathrm{COV}(\eta_2,\eta_3) + \cancel{\mathrm{COV}(\eta_2,\epsilon_3)}$$

$$\sigma_{y2y4} = \lambda^y_{43}\,\mathrm{COV}(\eta_2,\eta_3) + \cancel{\mathrm{COV}(\eta_2,\epsilon_4)}$$

$$\sigma_{y2y5} = \mathrm{COV}(\eta_2,\eta_4)$$

$$\sigma_{y2y6} = \mathrm{COV}(\eta_2,\eta_5) + \cancel{\mathrm{COV}(\eta_2,\epsilon_6)}$$

$$\sigma_{y2y7} = \lambda^y_{75}\,\mathrm{COV}(\eta_2,\eta_5) + \cancel{\mathrm{COV}(\eta_2,\epsilon_7)}$$

$$\sigma_{y3y4} = \lambda^y_{43}\,\mathrm{VAR}(\eta_3) + \cancel{\theta^{\epsilon}_{34}} + \cancel{\mathrm{COV}(\eta_3,\epsilon_4)} + \lambda^y_{43}\,\cancel{\mathrm{COV}(\eta_3,\epsilon_3)}$$

$$\sigma_{y3y5} = \mathrm{COV}(\eta_3,\eta_4) + \cancel{\mathrm{COV}(\eta_4,\epsilon_3)}$$

$$\sigma_{y3y6} = \mathrm{COV}(\eta_3,\eta_5) + \theta^{\epsilon}_{36} + \cancel{\mathrm{COV}(\eta_5,\epsilon_3)} + \cancel{\mathrm{COV}(\eta_3,\epsilon_6)}$$

$$\sigma_{y3y7} = \lambda^y_{75}\,\mathrm{COV}(\eta_3,\eta_5) + \cancel{\theta^{\epsilon}_{37}} + \cancel{\mathrm{COV}(\eta_3,\epsilon_7)} + \lambda^y_{75}\,\cancel{\mathrm{COV}(\eta_5,\epsilon_3)}$$

$$\sigma_{y4y5} = \lambda^y_{43}\,\mathrm{COV}(\eta_3,\eta_4) + \cancel{\mathrm{COV}(\eta_4,\epsilon_4)}$$

$$\sigma_{y4y6} = \lambda^y_{43}\,\mathrm{COV}(\eta_3,\eta_5) + \cancel{\theta^{\epsilon}_{46}} + \lambda^y_{43}\,\cancel{\mathrm{COV}(\eta_3,\epsilon_6)} + \cancel{\mathrm{COV}(\eta_5,\epsilon_4)}$$

$$\sigma_{y4y7} = \lambda^y_{43}\,\lambda^y_{75}\,\mathrm{COV}(\eta_3,\eta_5) + \theta^{\epsilon}_{47} + \lambda^y_{43}\,\cancel{\mathrm{COV}(\eta_3,\epsilon_7)} + \lambda^y_{75}\,\cancel{\mathrm{COV}(\eta_5,\epsilon_4)}$$

$$\sigma_{y5y6} = \mathrm{COV}(\eta_4,\eta_5) + \cancel{\mathrm{COV}(\eta_4,\epsilon_6)}$$

$$\sigma_{y5y7} = \lambda^y_{75}\,\mathrm{COV}(\eta_4,\eta_5) + \cancel{\mathrm{COV}(\eta_4,\epsilon_7)}$$

$$\sigma_{y6y7} = \lambda^y_{75}\,\mathrm{VAR}(\eta_5) + \cancel{\theta^{\epsilon}_{67}} + \cancel{\mathrm{COV}(\eta_5,\epsilon_7)} + \lambda^y_{75}\,\cancel{\mathrm{COV}(\eta_5,\epsilon_6)}$$

While these equations may seem overwhelming, assumptions that errors and factors are uncorrelated, and that some pairs of errors are uncorrelated result in a significant simplification. When these simplifications are added to the equations (as indicated by the lines crossing out some terms), a number of parameters are easily proven identified since they are exactly equal to a covariance between observed variables. These are ϕ_{11}, VAR(η_1), VAR(η_2), VAR(η_4), and all covariances between latent variables except for COV(η_3,η_5).

The loadings are proven identified as follows:

$$\lambda^y_{43} = \sigma_{x1y4} \div \sigma_{x1y3}$$

$$\lambda^y_{75} = \sigma_{x1y7} \div \sigma_{x1y6}$$

Then using the fact that the loadings are identified, the remaining covariance between latent variables is proven identified:

$$\text{COV}(\eta_3,\eta_5) = \sigma_{y3y7} \div \lambda^y_{75}$$

Identifying the remaining parameters follows readily:

$$\begin{aligned}
\text{VAR}(\eta_3) &= \sigma_{y3y4} \div \lambda^y_{43} \\
\theta^\epsilon_{36} &= \sigma_{y3y6} - \text{COV}(\eta_3,\eta_5) \\
\theta^\epsilon_{47} &= \sigma_{y4y7} - \lambda^y_{43}\lambda^y_{75}\text{COV}(\eta_3,\eta_5) \\
\text{VAR}(\eta_5) &= \sigma_{y6y7} \div \lambda^y_{75} \\
\theta^\epsilon_{33} &= \sigma_{y3y3} - \text{VAR}(\eta_3) \\
\theta^\epsilon_{44} &= \sigma_{y4y4} - \lambda^{y\,2}_{43}\ \text{VAR}(\eta_3) \\
\theta^\epsilon_{66} &= \sigma_{y6y6} - \text{VAR}(\eta_5) \\
\theta^\epsilon_{77} &= \sigma_{y7y7} - \lambda^{y\,2}_{75}\ \text{VAR}(\eta_5)
\end{aligned}$$

All parameters in the measurement model and all variances and covariances of the latent variables have been proven identified. Since the covariances between the latent variables are identified, the parameters of the structural model can be proved identified with exactly the same arguments as used in Example 3.2 of Chapter 3. //

Example 4.2: identification. As in the last example, the structural component of this model is identified if the variances and covariances of the latent variables are identified. The proof of this is identical to the proof of identification in Example 3.3. Since $\mathbf{x} = \boldsymbol{\xi}$, $\boldsymbol{\Phi}$ is equal to the matrix of variances and covariances of the x's. Hence, $\boldsymbol{\Phi}$ is identified. The measurement equations for the y's are

$$y_1 = \eta_1 + \epsilon_1 \qquad y_2 = \lambda^y_{21}\eta_1 + \epsilon_2$$

$$y_3 = \eta_2 + \epsilon_3 \qquad y_4 = \lambda^y_{42}\eta_2 + \epsilon_4$$

Since the ξ's are assumed to be uncorrelated with the ϵ's, the covariances between the η's and ϵ's are easily proven identified. For example, multiplying the equation for y_1 by $\xi_1 = x_1$ and taking expectations results in $E(y_1x_1) = E(\eta_1x_1) + E(\epsilon_1x_1)$, or $\sigma_{y_1x_1} = COV(\eta_1,x_1) = COV(\eta_1,\xi_1)$. The covariance equations for the y's are

$$\sigma_{y_1y_1} = VAR(\eta_1) + \theta^\epsilon_{11} \qquad \sigma_{y_2y_2} = \lambda^{y\,2}_{21}\, VAR(\eta_1) + \theta^\epsilon_{22}$$
$$\sigma_{y_3y_3} = VAR(\eta_2) + \theta^\epsilon_{33} \qquad \sigma_{y_4y_4} = \lambda^{y\,2}_{42}\, VAR(\eta_2) + \theta^\epsilon_{44}$$
$$\sigma_{y_1y_2} = \lambda^y_{21} VAR(\eta_1) \qquad \sigma_{y_1y_3} = COV(\eta_1,\eta_2) + \theta^\epsilon_{13}$$
$$\sigma_{y_1y_4} = \lambda^y_{42} COV(\eta_1,\eta_2) \qquad \sigma_{y_2y_3} = \lambda^y_{21} COV(\eta_1,\eta_2)$$
$$\sigma_{y_2y_4} = \lambda^y_{21}\lambda^y_{42} COV(\eta_1,\eta_2) + \theta^\epsilon_{24} \qquad \sigma_{y_3y_4} = \lambda^y_{42} VAR(\eta_2)$$

where assumed zero covariances have been left out of the equations. These ten equations contain eleven independent parameters; hence the equations cannot be solved for the parameters. If the measurement model for the y's was to be analyzed separately from the rest of the model, the model would not be identified. *But in the covariance structure model, identification of each parameter can use the information from the entire model.* In this case the covariance equations for y_2 and x_1, and y_4 and x_1 allow us to prove that the parameters for the measurement model for the y's are identified. The covariance equations are

$$\sigma_{y_2x_1} = \lambda^y_{21} COV(\eta_1,\xi_1)$$
$$\sigma_{y_4x_1} = \lambda^y_{42} COV(\eta_2,\xi_1)$$

Since $COV(\eta_1,\xi_1)$ and $COV(\eta_2,\xi_1)$ are identified, the two loadings can be solved for. Given that the loadings are identified, the variances of the η's are also identified:

$$VAR(\eta_1) = \sigma_{y_1y_2} \div \lambda^y_{21}$$
$$VAR(\eta_2) = \sigma_{y_3y_4} \div \lambda^y_{42}$$

This allows the identification of θ^ϵ_{11}, θ^ϵ_{22}, θ^ϵ_{33}, and θ^ϵ_{44}. The remaining parameters are proven identified as follows:

$$COV(\eta_1,\eta_2) = \sigma_{y_1y_4} \div \lambda^y_{42}$$
$$\theta^\epsilon_{13} = \sigma_{y_1y_3} - COV(\eta_1,\eta_2)$$
$$\theta^\epsilon_{24} = \sigma_{y_2y_4} - \lambda^y_{21}\lambda^y_{42} COV(\eta_1,\eta_2)$$

Each parameter has been solved for in terms of the variances and covariances of the observed variables; hence the model is identified. Many of the parameters are overidentified, which the reader should attempt to verify by solving some of the parameters in different ways. //

Proving identification by solving for the parameters involves many steps, many parameters, and many places to make errors. To avoid such errors it is suggested that as a first step the measurement and structural equations of the model be written down with lower case Roman letters taking the place of the subscripted Greek parameters. This reduces the chances of incorrectly transcribing subscripts. Second, make a list of all of the covariance equations, using the Roman letters rather than the Greek. Third, make a list of all parameters that need to be identified. Fourth, make several copies of these lists, to be used in verifying your work. Fifth, as you prove that a parameter is identified, mark it as identified on the list of parameters and cross it out in each occurrence in the covariance equations. Proceed in this fashion until all parameters are proven identified. Sixth, wait a day and repeat step five without consulting your earlier proof. While this may seem to be a great deal of effort, remember that if an attempt is made to estimate a model that is not identified, all resulting analyses are meaningless.

Estimation

Once identification has been established, estimation can proceed. The covariance structure model can be estimated by any of the full-information methods discussed earlier: unweighted least squares (ULS), generalized least squares (GLS), and maximum likelihood (ML). Estimates are those values of the parameters that minimize the difference between the observed covariance matrix S and the predicted covariance matrix $\hat{\Sigma}$, where the definition of the difference between the two matrices is determined by the method of estimation. Estimating the covariance structure model adds no new difficulties to those discussed in *CFA*, the only difference being that the estimated covariance matrix is defined as follows (see equation 4.4):

$$\hat{\boldsymbol{\Sigma}} = \left[\begin{array}{c|c} \hat{\boldsymbol{\Lambda}}_y \hat{\ddot{\mathbf{B}}}^{-1}(\hat{\boldsymbol{\Gamma}}\hat{\boldsymbol{\Phi}}\hat{\boldsymbol{\Gamma}}' + \hat{\boldsymbol{\Psi}})\hat{\ddot{\mathbf{B}}}'^{-1}\hat{\boldsymbol{\Lambda}}_y' + \hat{\boldsymbol{\Theta}}_\epsilon & \hat{\boldsymbol{\Lambda}}_y \hat{\ddot{\mathbf{B}}}^{-1}\hat{\boldsymbol{\Gamma}}\hat{\boldsymbol{\Phi}}\hat{\boldsymbol{\Lambda}}_x' \\ \hline \hat{\boldsymbol{\Lambda}}_x \hat{\boldsymbol{\Phi}}\hat{\boldsymbol{\Gamma}}'\hat{\ddot{\mathbf{B}}}'^{-1}\hat{\boldsymbol{\Lambda}}_y' & \hat{\boldsymbol{\Lambda}}_x \hat{\boldsymbol{\Phi}}\hat{\boldsymbol{\Lambda}}_x' + \hat{\boldsymbol{\Theta}}_\delta \end{array}\right]$$

Without making any assumptions about the distribution of the observed variables, ULS can be shown to be consistent. The advantage of not requiring distributional assumptions is offset by ULS being scale dependent and not having any statistical tests associated with it. If the observed variables have a multivariate normal distribution, both GLS and ML have desirable asymptotic properties. ML is approximately unbiased, has as small a sampling variance as any other estimator, and is approximately normally distributed. GLS is asymptotically equivalent to ML. Greater detail on the properties of these estimators can be found in *CFA*.

Covariance structure models tend to have more parameters than factor analytic or structural equation models (although this is not necessarily so). This poses the practical problem that it may be expensive to compute the estimates. Each method of estimation proceeds iteratively, successively finding better and better estimates of the parameters. The first step in the iteration requires start values. The rate of convergence to the final estimates can be greatly speeded up if the start values are chosen accurately. A particularly useful feature of LISREL V is that start values are selected by the program for many types of models (Jöreskog and Sörbom, 1981: I.32).

Assessment of Fit

No additional techniques are required to assess the fit of the covariance structure model. Accordingly, this section only reviews the techniques presented in earlier chapters and in *CFA*.

Examining values of the parameters. The parameters from the measurement component of the model can be examined and interpreted in exactly the same way as the parameters of the factor analytic model. Similarly, the parameters in the structural component of the covariance structure model can be interpreted as in the structural equation model. Negative variances, correlations greater than one, and unreasonably large parameter estimates all signal that something is wrong. Possible problems are misspecification, a pairwise covariance matrix, an unidentified or nearly unidentified model, and/or faulty control cards for the software being used.

The signs of parameters should be carefully examined. Some programs refer to our **B** as "BETA," while others refer to our $\ddot{\mathbf{B}}$ as "BETA." It is important to realize which definition is being used. If equality constraints are being imposed on parameters from two different matrices, the "equal" parameters may be forced to have opposite signs. For example, in using LISREL V the constraint that β_{ij} (not $\ddot{\beta}_{ij}$) equals γ_{mn}, results in the imposed equality: $\beta_{ij} = -\gamma_{mn}$. Unless the estimates are examined with care, it is easy to miss such problems.

Variances and covariances of the parameters. The variances of the parameter estimates can be computed with GLS and ML estimation. Under assumptions of the normality of the observed variables, the parameter estimates are asymptotically normally distributed, allowing z-tests of hypotheses that individual parameters are equal to some constant. From the covariances between estimates it is possible to compute correlations between estimates. Large correlations indicate that it is difficult to distinguish between the two parameters. This is the problem of empirical underidentification discussed in *CFA*.

Chi-square goodness-of-fit tests. Under the assumptions of normality, ML and GLS estimation provide a chi-square test of the proposed model against the alternative model that $\boldsymbol{\Sigma}$ is unconstrained. Large values of the chi-square relative to degrees of freedom indicate that the model does not provide an adequate fit of the data. Degrees of freedom for the chi-square test are $df = \frac{1}{2}(p + q)(p + q + 1) - t$, where t is the number of independent parameters being estimated.

A difference of chi-square test can be used to compare nested models. If M_1 can be obtained from M_2 by constraining one or more of the parameters in M_2, M_1 is said to be nested in M_2. If M_1 with X_1^2 and df_1 is nested in M_2 with X_2^2 and df_2, for large samples $X^2 = X_1^2 - X_2^2$ is distributed as chi-square with $df = df_1 - df_2$. Large values of the chi-square relative to the degrees of freedom indicates that the additional constraints imposed in the restricted model M_1 should be rejected.

Effects of sample size on hypothesis testing. Hypothesis testing with either the chi-square test or the z-test is affected by the size of the sample being analysed.[9] Superficially the effects of sample size on tests with the chi-square statistic appear to be contradictory to the effects of sample size on z-tests of individual parameters. For example, as sample size gets larger, it is more likely that a given model will be rejected as inadequate to reproduce the observed covariance matrix (i.e., the probability level gets larger). At the same time, the statistical significance of individual parameters tends to increase (i.e., the probability level gets smaller). These results are, however, perfectly reasonable.

With larger sample sizes sampling variability decreases. Differences between two samples are likely to be smaller due to the larger sample size. Since there is less sampling variability, a given lack of fit is more likely due to the null hypothesis being false (e.g., a parameter is not equal to the hypothesized value) than to sampling variability (e.g., a parameter is not equal to the hypothesized value due to peculiarities of a particular sample). Consequently, as sample size increases, smaller and smaller differences between the estimated value of a parameter and hypothesized value become significant.

A similar result holds for the chi-square test. One way of viewing the chi-square test is as a simultaneous test of the differences between the observed and predicted covariances among observed variables. As sample size increases, smaller and smaller differences between observed and predicted covariances become statistically significant, in the same way that smaller and smaller differences between estimated values of individual parameters and hypothesized values of those parameters become statistically significant.

As a consequence, in very large samples almost any model with positive degrees of freedom is likely to be rejected as providing a statistically unacceptable fit. This is true even when the rejected model is what Bentler and Bonett (1980: 591) call "minimally false." Their idea of a minimally false model refers to a model that is rejected on the basis of a chi-square test when the differences between the elements of the observed covariance matrix **S** and the covariance matrix predicted by the model $\hat{\Sigma}$ are trivial. They conclude that even though a better model might be able to explain these deviations, the original model might explain all that is of substantive importance. Jöreskog and Sörbom (1981: I.38-39) put the same idea somewhat differently, indicating that the statistical problem is not one of testing a particular hypothesis, but of determining whether a model provides an adequate fit of the data.

The precise relationship between test statistics and sample size is very simple. For ML and GLS estimation, the chi-square statistic is computed as $(N - 1)\,\Delta$, where N is the sample size and Δ is a quantity that depends on the covariance matrix for the observed variables but not the sample size. For example, assume that two samples are fit to the same model. Sample 1 has N_1 observations and sample 2 has N_2 observations. Assume that both samples have exactly the same covariance matrix for the observed variables. Since Δ is not a function of sample size, Δ would be the same for both samples. The chi-squares would differ, however, due to the differences in sample size. Specifically, $X_1^2 = (N_1 - 1)\Delta$ and $X_2^2 = (N_2 - 1)\Delta$. The relationship between the two chi-squares would be

$$X_2^2 = X_1^2 \frac{N_2 - 1}{N_1 - 1}$$

A similar relationship exists between sample size and the magnitude of the z-statistic. Consider any specific parameter, call it ω. The variance of the sampling distribution of $\hat{\omega}$ is equal to $[\Delta/(N-1)]$, where Δ is a value that does not depend on the sample size. Once again, assume that two samples are fit to the same model. Sample 1 has N_1 observations and sample 2 has N_2 observations. Assume that both samples had exactly the same covariance matrix for the observed variables. Since Δ is not a function of sample size, Δ would be the same for the analysis of both samples. The variances of the sampling distribution would differ, however, due to the differences in sample size. Specifically, $\hat{\sigma}_1^2 = \Delta/(N_1 - 1)$ and $\hat{\sigma}_2^2 = \Delta/(N_2 - 1)$. The relationship between the two variances would be

$$\hat{\sigma}_2^2 = \hat{\sigma}_1^2 \frac{N_1 - 1}{N_2 - 1}$$

The formula for the z-statistic is $z = (\hat{\omega} - \omega^*)/\hat{\sigma}$, where ω^* is a constant that ω is hypothesized to equal. Since $\hat{\omega}$ and ω^* are not affected by changes in the sample size, the effect of changes in sample size on the z-statistic is

$$z_2 = z_1 \sqrt{\frac{N_2 - 1}{N_1 - 1}}$$

where z_1 is the z-statistic for the sample of size N_1, and z_2 is the z-statistic for the sample of size N_2.

Modification indices. If a model does not fit adequately, a specification search can be conducted. Parameters can be dropped from the model if they are not significantly different from zero. Alternatively, parameters can be added to the model. By relaxing the parameter with the maximum value of the modification index (defined in Chapter 3 and *CFA*), the greatest improvement in fit is obtained. In specification searches several points should be kept in mind. First, all models considered must be proven identified. Second, the chosen model cannot be formally tested with a z-test or a chi-square test. Since the model was selected by the data, it cannot be tested with the same data. Third, the search should be guided by substantive considerations. Even if the model initially suggested by substantive theory is rejected, there are generally some parameters that are definitely required on the basis of past research, and some parameters that make no sense to include (e.g., in a panel model letting variables at time 2 affect variables at time 1). These parameters should not be dropped or added, respectively, to improve the fit of the model.

Derivative parameters. It is sometimes useful to compute additional parameters derived from those estimated for the model. Correlations among the latent variables can be computed from the covariances that have been estimated. For example, the correlation between ξ_i and ξ_j can be computed as $\rho_{ij} = \phi_{ij} \div \sqrt{\phi_{ii}\phi_{jj}}$, where the ϕ's are elements of $\mathbf{\Phi}$. To evaluate multiple indicators of latent variables, reliabilities can be computed. (See *CFA* for details on the computation and interpretation of reliabilities.) Within the structural component of the model, the coefficient of determination can be computed for each equation. In the equation predicting η_i, the coefficient of determination is equal to $R^2 = (s_{ii} - \hat{\psi}_{ii})/s_{ii}$. Our discussion of the coefficient of determination in Chapter 3 applies here as well. Any of the parameters considered in our earlier discussion of the factor model and the structural equation model can be applied directly to the more general covariance structure model.

These techniques are now illustrated with our two examples.

Example 4.1: estimation and hypothesis testing. Table 4.2 contains the results from the ML estimation of six models for the sociogenesis of psychological disorder. Model M_d corresponds most closely to the model estimated by Wheaton (1978).[10] Models M_a, M_b, and M_c are substantively unrealistic, but are useful for illustrating a number of points in hypothesis testing and model specification. Models M_e and M_f extend Wheaton's model by incorporating serially correlated errors.

Model M_a assumes that all errors in equations are uncorrelated, that all errors in variables are uncorrelated, and that no parameters are constrained to be equal. The fit of this model is poor, with a chi-square of 142.6 and 13 degrees of freedom. Model M_b adds two sets of substantively reasonable equality constraints (1) $\beta_{21} = \beta_{42}$, indicating that the stability of SES is constant over time; and (2) $\lambda^y_{43} = \lambda^y_{75}$, indicating that the loadings on the psychophysiological symptoms subscale are equal at both points in time. Imposing these constraints frees two degrees of freedom and increases the chi-square by 4.84. This allows a test of the joint hypothesis H_0: $\beta_{21} = \beta_{42}$ and $\lambda^y_{43} = \lambda^y_{75}$ in M_a. The appropriate test statistic is $X^2 = X^2_b - X^2_a = 4.84$ with $df = df_b - df_a = 2$ degrees of freedom. The hypothesis cannot be rejected at the .05 level.

TABLE 4.2

FIML Estimates of Six Covariance Structure Models for the Sociogenesis of Psychological Disorder (Models M_a to M_f)

Parameter	M_a	M_b	M_c	M_d	M_e	M_f
γ_{11}	0.294***	0.294***	0.294***	0.294***	0.294***	0.294***
β_{21}	0.877***	0.862[a]***	0.861[a]***	0.860[a]***	0.894[a]***	0.893[a]***
γ_{21}	0.026	0.031*	0.031*	0.031*	0.021	0.021
β_{31}	–.010***	–.010***	–.010***	–.008***	–.008***	–.006***
γ_{31}	–.002	–.002	–.002	0.000	–.000	–.000
β_{42}	0.844***	0.862[a]***	0.861[a]***	0.860[a]***	0.894[a]***	0.893[a]***
β_{43}	0.052	0.160	–.002	–1.495***	–.846**	–.916*
γ_{41}	0.061***	0.056***	0.055***	0.053***	0.044**	0.045***
β_{52}	–.000	0.000	–.000	0.000	–.000	0.001
β_{53}	0.601***	0.661***	0.619***	0.672***	0.649***	0.949***
γ_{51}	–.002	–.002	–.002	–.000	–.000	0.000
COR(ζ_3, ζ_2)	–	–	–	0.293***	0.269***	0.243***
COR(ζ_4, ζ_2)	–	–	–	–	–.276***	–.268***
COR(ζ_5, ζ_3)	–	–	–	–	–	–.389**
COR(ζ_5, ζ_4)	–	–	–	0.186***	0.181***	0.122***
λ^y_{43}	0.211***	0.244[b]***	0.268[b]***	0.485[b]***	0.443[b]***	0.503[b]***
λ^y_{75}	0.271***	0.244[b]***	0.268[b]***	0.485[b]***	0.443[b]***	0.503[b]***
REL(η_3, y_3)	0.823	0.746	0.676	0.367	0.408	0.361
REL(η_3, y_4)	0.250	0.304	0.331	0.588	0.546	0.625
REL(η_5, y_6)	0.740	0.792	0.729	0.413	0.446	0.392
REL(η_5, y_7)	0.407	0.355	0.394	0.730	0.657	0.749
COR(ϵ_3, ϵ_6)	–	–	0.278	0.465***	0.457***	0.469***
COR(ϵ_4, ϵ_7)	–	–	0.140	–.364**	–.200	–.386**
Chi-square	142.65	147.49	131.00	89.84	45.37	40.79
df	13	15	13	11	10	9
prob	0.00	0.00	0.00	0.00	0.00	0.00

NOTE: Roman letters indicate that coefficients are constrained to be equal. * indicates significance at .10 (.20) level for one-(two-)tailed test; ** at .05 (.10) level for one-(two-) tailed test; *** at .025 (.050) level for one-(two-) tailed test. See Figure 4.1 or text for specific meanings of coefficients. All coefficients are unstandardized and estimated by FIML (full-information maximum likelihood). Estimates were computed with LISREL V.

M_c relaxes θ^{ϵ}_{36} and θ^{ϵ}_{47}, the covariances between errors in the same measures at two points in time. The motivation for relaxing these parameters is that if, for example, the psychological symptoms subscale contained measurement error at time 2 (y_3), it is possible that similar sources of measurement error are present at time 3 (y_6). That is, $\theta^{\epsilon}_{36} \neq 0$; similarly, for psychological symptions (y_4 and y_7), $\theta^{\epsilon}_{47} \neq 0$. Freeing these parameters uses two degrees of freedom and decreases the chi-square by 16.5. Thus the hypothesis H_0: $\theta^{\epsilon}_{36} = \theta^{\epsilon}_{47} = 0$ can be rejected at any conventional level of significance.

Models M_a and M_c each use the same number of parameters to reproduce the covariance matrix, with M_c being more successful, as indicated by the smaller chi-square. Whether this difference of 11.7 in the chi-square is statistically significant cannot be formally tested, since M_a and M_c are not nested. However, given the substantively more realistic characteristics of M_c, it would be the preferable model.

M_d adds same-time correlated errors in equations to M_c. Freeing ψ_{23} and ψ_{45} results in a significant improvement in fit, with a change in chi-square of 41.2 and a loss of two degrees of freedom. While the overall fit of the model is still not statistically acceptable ($X^2 = 89.8$ with df = 11), it is comparable to the fit obtained by Wheaton for a similar model.

Model M_d does not provide an acceptable fit, even though it is the model suggested by theory. The maximum modification index for M_d is for the coefficient ψ_{24}, with a value of 36.6. ψ_{24} corresponds to a serial correlation between the equations predicting SES at time 2 and SES at time 3. Its presence is reasonable given that it is likely that the model has excluded other variables that are important for explaining SES. M_e frees this covariance, reducing the chi-square by 44.5 with a loss of one degree of freedom, a significant improvement in fit. M_f extends this reasoning by adding a serial correlation between the two equations predicting psychological disorders. While the improvement in fit is not as large, it is significant at the .05 level.

Model M_f still does not provide a statistically adequate fit with a chi-square of 40.8 and nine degrees of freedom. The maximum modification index in M_f is 17.37 for θ^{ϵ}_{26}. However, since the variance of ϵ_6 is constrained to equal zero, it makes no sense to free the covariance between ϵ_6 and ϵ_2. This illustrates the point that in using the modification index it must be kept in mind that there is no gain if the fit of a model is improved by adding meaningless parameters.

The results of greatest interest are contained in the structural portion of the model. They are nearly identical to those obtained in the structural equation model of Chapter 3 (see M_b in Table 3.4), with one important difference. The path from psychological disorder at time 2 to SES at time 3 is statistically significant in M_d, while it isn't significant in the earlier structural equation model or in Wheaton's (1978: 396) original article. Substantively this path is important, indicating what Wheaton called a social selection effect—"a retardation in status attainment between [time 2] and [time 3] attributable to disorder" (Wheaton, 1978: 392). This type of effect is in contrast to social causation effects as indicated by the path from SES at time 1 to psychological disorder at time 2. The analysis here finds evidence of both social causation (as indicated by the structural parameter β_{31}) and social selection (as indicated by the structural parameter β_{43}), whereas Wheaton found only an effect of social causation.

The reader should not take the differences between these findings and those of Wheaton as a critique of the original analysis. In adapting Wheaton's model for the present purposes, a number of simplifying assumptions were made. While these simplifications are ones that a researcher might impose in order to model the sociogenesis of psychological disorder, they are nonetheless simplifications. The fact that a substantive difference is found reflects a cost of the great power of the covariance structure model. Because of the complexity of the model, many decisions in the specification of a model have to be made that are not dictated by substantive considerations. These decisions can affect the substantive conclusions drawn from the model. Because of full-information estimation, making changes in one part of the model can affect results in a seemingly quite different part of the model. For example, in moving from M_c to M_d, the social selection effect (β_{43}) changed from being statistically nonsignificant to being significant. Also, as shown with M_e and M_f, the introduction of other reasonable parameters can affect other parameters in the model.

The most useful information in the measurement component of the model is the reliabilities of the various measures. In models M_a through M_c the measures of psychological symptoms (y_3 and y_6) are the most reliable. However, in M_d the measures of psychophysiological symptoms (y_4 and y_7) are the most reliable. Further, in moving from M_c to M_d, the covariances in errors in measurement become statistically significant. //

Example 4.2: estimation and hypothesis testing. The second example extends Example 3.3 by adding two indicators for each of the endogenous variables (compare Figures 3.2 and 4.2). In Chapter 3 it was argued that, given the symmetry between the effects for the respondent and the respondent's friend, corresponding parameters should be constrained to be equal. For example, the effect of the respondent's IQ on the respondent's ambitions (γ_{12}) should equal the effect of the friend's IQ on the friend's ambitions (γ_{25}). Similarly, the loading of the respondent's occupational aspirations (y_2) on the respondent's ambitions (η_1) should equal the loading of the friend's occupational aspirations (y_4) on the friend's ambitions (η_2). That is, $\lambda^y_{21} = \lambda^y_{42}$. The resulting model is estimated in Table 4.3 and is referred to as M_a. The overall fit of the model is quite good, with a chi-square of 30.6 with 24 degrees of freedom (prob = 0.17).

The results from the structural component of the model are essentially the same as those obtained in Example 3.3. Any changes are due to the new dependent variables, which are now latent variables based on two measures of aspirations. For both respondents and friends, measures of educational aspirations are more reliable indicators of ambition than are measures of occupational aspirations.

Educational aspirations are measured for both friends and respondents. Given that the same measure is used twice, it is possible that errors in measurement are correlated—that is, $\theta^\epsilon_{13} \neq 0$. Similarly, errors in the measurement of occupational aspirations might be correlated: $\theta^\epsilon_{24} \neq 0$. Model M_b incorporates this change. Freeing two parameters, thus giving up two degrees of freedom, results in a change in the chi-square of 14.5, a very significant improvement in fit. The values of the other parameters in the model are not appreciably different from those in M_a, and the overall fit of the model is improved with a chi-square of 16.1 with 22 degrees of freedom (prob = 0.81). //

Summary

The covariance structure model is complex, and our treatment of it has been all too brief. It is easy to lose sight of its potential in the complexities of the mathematical development. Perhaps the best way to master the model is to study and reproduce substantive applications of the model. The following books and articles are recommended for this purpose: Alwin and Jackson (1982), Bagozzi (1981), Bielby et al. (1977), Bynner (1981), Dalton (1982), Jöreskog (1974, 1978), Judd and Milburn (1980), Kenny (1979), Kessler and Greenberg (1981), Krehbiel and

TABLE 4.3

FIML Estimates of Two Covariance Structure Models for Peer Influences on Aspirations (Models M_a and M_b)

Parameter	M_a	M_b
β_{12}	0.202[a]***	0.201[a]***
γ_{11}	0.166[b]***	0.170[b]***
γ_{12}	0.307[c]***	0.310[c]***
γ_{13}	0.233[d]***	0.235[d]***
γ_{14}	0.071[e]***	0.074[e]***
β_{21}	0.202[a]***	0.201[a]***
γ_{23}	0.071[e]**	0.074[e]***
γ_{24}	0.233[d]***	0.235[d]***
γ_{25}	0.307[c]***	0.310[c]***
γ_{26}	0.166[b]***	0.170[b]***
COR (ζ_1,ζ_2)	-.065	-.162
λ^y_{21}	0.936[f]***	0.908[f]***
λ^y_{42}	0.936[f]***	0.908[f]***
REL(η_1, y_1)	0.450	0.475
REL(η_1, y_2)	0.394	0.392
REL(η_2, y_3)	0.464	0.490
REL(η_2, y_4)	0.406	0.403
COR(ϵ_2, ϵ_4)	–	0.267***
COR(ϵ_1, ϵ_3)	–	0.065
Chi-square	30.63	16.10
df	24	22
prob	0.17	0.81

NOTE: Roman letters indicate that coefficients are constrained to be equal. * indicates significance at .10 (.20) level for one-(two-)tailed test; ** at .05 (.10) level for one-(two-)tailed-test; *** at .025 (.050) level for one-(two-)tailed test. See Figure 4.2 or text for specific meanings of coefficients. All coefficients are unstandardized and estimated by FIML (full-information maximum likelihood). Estimates were computed with LISREL V.

Niemi (1982), Long (1981), Sullivan and Feldman (1979), and Wheaton et al. (1977). The manuals for LISREL IV and LISREL V also contain a number of useful applications (Jöreskog and Sörbom, 1978, 1981).

5. CONCLUSION

Factor models, regression and correlation models, multiple indicator models, and second-order factor models, among others, can each be incorporated into the common framework of the covariance structure model. Yet, even with the power and flexibility of the covariance structure model, a number of limitations remain in the form of the model that we have presented. No provision has been made for comparing models across groups. For ML and GLS, all observed variables are assumed to be normally distributed, even though in practice dichotomous and ordinal variables are common. All models are assumed to be linear, and all constraints are either exclusion constraints or simple equality constraints. A number of researchers are working to extend the model along these lines. These include P. Bentler, K. Jöreskog, R. McDonald, B. Múthen, D. Sörbom, and D. Weeks. Advances are being published regularly in such journals as *Psychometrika, Multivariate Behavioral Research, British Journal of Statistical and Mathematical Psychology,* and *Econometrica.* While a detailed presentation of these important advances is beyond the scope of this monograph, a brief overview may help the reader to pursue them further.

Group comparisons. Fundamental research questions often involve testing for the presence of group differences. Does the effect of variable x on variable y differ for males and females? Are there differences between treatment and control groups? Extensions of the covariance structure model to deal with group comparisons have been made primarily by K. Jöreskog and D. Sörbom and are incorporated in LISREL IV and LISREL V (Jöreskog and Sörbom, 1978, 1981), although models by Bentler and Weeks (1979) and McDonald (1980) can also incorporate group differences. Analysis essentially involves simultaneously estimating covariance structure models for each group and comparing the effects of various constraints across groups. Applications of this approach include Sörbom (1982) and Magidson (1977).

Analysis of discrete data. For estimation by ML or GLS, variables are assumed to be approximately normal. If data are highly nonnormal, ULS estimation is suggested. If the variables are dichotomous or ordinal, and they can be assumed to reflect unobserved variables that are continuous, then polychoric, tetrachoric, and polyserial correlations (see Guilford and Fruchter, 1978) can be used as input for estimation by ULS. Jöreskog and Sörbom (1981: chap. IV) have demonstrated the application of this approach using LISREL V.

More complex structures and constraints. Earlier it was noted that in the most general case the covariance structure model can be considered as a model that explains covariances among observed variables as *any* function of a set of parameters (assuming the resulting model is identified). Such an extremely general model has been discussed by McDonald (1978) and Jöreskog (1978), although for practical purposes such general formulations cannot be applied. Somewhat less general models that have important practical applications have been developed by Bentler (Bentler, 1976; Bentler and Weeks, 1979) and McDonald (1980). The most important advantages are their ability to include a wider variety of constraints on parameters and to incorporate more complex measurement models.

Software for the covariance structure model. Each of these enhancements of the covariance structure model, as well as the basic covariance structure model, requires sophisticated software. Indeed, each breakthrough in the development of the covariance structure model has required a corresponding breakthrough in statistical software. Thus it is appropriate to conclude with a brief discussion of the programs that are available.

The first program developed for the covariance structure model was LISREL, written by K. G. Joreskog and M. van Thillo (1972) while at Educational Testing Service (ETS). The first version of this program is limited by a cumbersome set of control cards and the inability to compute standard errors. Its greatest advantages were being the first program available and being distributed without charge from ETS (although it is no longer available). A second version of LISREL, known as LISREL II, included the calculation of standard errors. The reader is warned that some copies of this version contain serious errors. The most recent version of LISREL, LISREL V, is distributed by

International Educational Services (1525 East 53rd Street, Suite 829, Chicago, IL 60615). It has the advantages of a simple control language for setting up many types of models, computation of ULS and ML estimates, estimation of standard errors, computation of modification index, the ability to compute start values, and features that allow group comparisons and analysis of ordinal data.

MILS is a program developed by Ronald Schoenberg at the National Institute of Mental Health and can be obtained free of charge by writing to R. Schoenberg (National Institutes of Health, Building 31, Room 4C11, Bethesda, MD 20205). This program computes standard errors, GLS and ML estimates, allows group comparisons, and extends the covariance structure model to include some multiplicative models. The greatest limitations of this program are that control cards are more difficult to code, initial start values are not computed, and some useful statistics are not conputed (e.g., the modification index). It has the advantage of computing statistics to assess the stability of the solution and standard errors of the indirect effects.

EQS is a program developed by Peter Bentler. This program includes many of the features of LISREL V, including the ability to do group comparisons, the calculation of initial start values, and ULS and ML estimation. In addition, EQS allows more complex constraints, computes GLS estimates, and estimates the more general covariance structure model presented by Bentler and Weeks (1979).

COSAN is a program developed by R. McDonald and described in McDonald (1980). In some respects this appears to be the most general of the available programs, allowing the users to write FORTRAN subroutines to estimate nonstandard models.

Given the complexity of the covariance structure model and the programs used to estimate it, it is extremely easy to incorrectly set up the control cards for the program being used. Not only does this result in incorrect estimates (the incorrectness of which may be difficult to detect), but it can be expensive. Experience suggests that correct models are far cheaper to estimate than incorrect models. Until a user is familiar with a package, it is important to reestimate models that have been published in the literature to ensure an adequate understanding of the program being used. The examples given above can be used for this purpose; necessary data are given in the Appendix.

APPENDIX: COVARIANCE/CORRELATION MATRICES FOR EXAMPLES

TABLE A
Correlations and Standard Deviations from Wheaton, Hennepin Sample (N = 603)

Variables	*FSES*	*SES1*	*SES2*	*SES3*	*PSY2*	*PHY2*	*PSY3*	*PHY3*
FSES	1.000							
SES1	0.257	1.000						
SES2	0.248	0.882	1.000					
SES3	0.264	0.827	0.863	1.000				
PSY2	–.072	–.166	–.096	–.089	1.000			
PHY2	–.038	–.104	–.016	–.030	0.454	1.000		
PSY3	–.092	–.120	–.088	–.006	0.526	0.247	1.000	
PHY3	–.013	–.139	–.011	–.005	0.377	0.309	0.549	1.000
S.D.	19.98	22.82	22.85	22.69	1.45	0.555	1.38	0.503

SOURCE: Blair Wheaton, "Sociogenesis of Psychological Disorder," *American Sociological Review* Vol. 43, pp. 383-403 (Table 2).

VARIABLE IDENTIFICATIONS (followed by labels in Examples 3.2 and 4.1, respectively):

FSES: Father's socioeconomic status (ξ_1, x_1)
SES1: Socioeconomic status time 1 (η_1, y_1)
SES2: Socioeconomic status time 2 (η_2, y_2)
SES3: Socioeconomic status time 3 (η_4, y_5)
PSY2: Psychological disorders time 2 (η_3, y_3)
PHY2: Psychophysiological disorders time 2 (none, y_4)
PSY3: Psychological disorders time 3 (η_5, y_6)
PHY3: Psychophysiological disorders time 3 (none, y_7)

TABLE B

Data from Duncan, Haller, and Portes (N = 329)

Variables	*R-IQ*	*R-PASP*	*R-SES*	*R-OASP*	*R-EASP*	*F-IQ*	*F-PASP*	*F-SES*	*F-OASP*	*F-EASP*
R-IQ	1.0000									
R-PASP	0.1839	1.0000								
R-SES	0.2220	0.0489	1.0000							
R-OASP	0.4105	0.2137	0.3240	1.0000						
R-EASP	0.4043	0.2742	0.4047	0.6247	1.0000					
F-IQ	0.3355	0.0782	0.2302	0.2995	0.2863	1.0000				
F-PASP	0.1021	0.1147	0.0931	0.0760	0.0702	0.2087	1.0000			
F-SES	0.1861	0.0186	0.2707	0.2930	0.2407	0.2950	−.0438	1.0000		
F-OASP	0.2598	0.0839	0.2786	0.4216	0.3275	0.5007	0.1988	0.3607	1.0000	
F-EASP	0.2903	0.1124	0.3054	0.3269	0.3669	0.5191	0.2784	0.4105	0.6404	1.0000

SOURCE: O. D. Duncan, A. O. Haller, and A. Portes, "Peer Influences on Aspirations: A Reinterpretation," *American Journal of Sociology*, Vol. 74, pp. 119-137 (Table 1). Copyright © 1968 by The University of Chicago. Reprinted by permission of University of Chicago Press.

VARIABLE IDENTIFICATIONS (followed by labels in Examples 3.3 and 4.2 respectively):

R-IQ: Respondent's IQ (ξ_2, x_2)
R-PASP: Respondent's parental aspirations (ξ_1, x_1)
R-SES: Respondent's socioeconomic status (ξ_3, x_3)
R-OASP: Respondent's occupational aspirations (none, y_2)
R-EASP: Respondent's educational aspirations (η_1, y_1)
F-IQ: Friend's IQ (ξ_5, x_5)
F-PASP: Friend's parental aspirations (ξ_6, x_6)
F-SES: Friend's socioeconomic status (ξ_4, x_4)
F-OASP: Friend's occupational aspirations (none, y_4)
F-EASP: Friend's educational aspirations (η_2, y_3)

NOTES

1. The symbol "//" will be used to designate the end of an example.

2. More precisely, this condition means that **B** can be reduced to a triangular matrix by a suitable ordering of the equations.

3. The rank of a (r × c) matrix **X** is the size of the largest nonsingular submatrix of **X**. For example, the rank of

$$X = \begin{bmatrix} 1 & 2 \\ 3 & 4 \end{bmatrix}$$

is two since **X** is invertible; the rank of

$$X = \begin{bmatrix} 1 & 2 & 1 \\ 3 & 4 & 3 \\ 1 & 1 & 1 \end{bmatrix}$$

is two since **X** is not invertible, but

$$\begin{bmatrix} 1 & 2 \\ 3 & 4 \end{bmatrix}$$

is a (2 × 2) submatrix of X and is invertible.

4. Generalized least squares in this context refers to the single equation method of estimation sometimes referred to as Aitken's least squares.

5. This approach to estimation is different from that commonly found in the econometric literature. The ULS and GLS estimators do not correspond to any commonly found in that literature. ML corresponds to full information maximum likelihood. Malinvaud's (1970) approach to estimation is most similar to that presented here.

6. To say that a just-identified model has zero degrees of freedom is not to say that if a model has zero degrees of freedom it is just-identified. Unidentified models can have zero degrees of freedom.

7. For a more detailed treatment of direct, indirect, and total effects in causal modeling, see Wonnacott and Wonnacott (1981: 194-207), Alwin and Hauser (1975), and Duncan (1975).

8. While equality constraints are often justified in panel models, it may be unrealistic in this case. The Hennepin region was experiencing industrialization over the period from time 2 to time 3, but it was not from time 1 to time 2. Consequently, the stability of SES may have changed. I thank B. Wheaton for pointing this out. For purposes of illustration, however, it is useful to consider this constraint.

9. These results are not peculiar to the covariance structure model. They apply generally to problems of statistical inference.

10. Our specification differs from Wheaton's in two major respects. First, Wheaton assumes imperfect measurement of SES, while we assume perfect measurement. Second, we have assumed that the stability of SES over time is constant, while Wheaton did not (see Note 7). These modifications have been made for pedagogical reasons, rather than substantive reasons. The reader is encouraged to examine the original article (Wheaton, 1978).

REFERENCES

ALWIN, D. F. and R. M. HAUSER (1975) "The decomposition of effects in path analysis." American Sociological Review 40: 37-47.

ALWIN, D. F. and D. J. JACKSON (1982) "The statistical analysis of Kohn's measures of parental values," pp. 197-223 in H. Wold and K. Jöreskog (eds.) Systems Under Indirect Observation. New York: Elsevier North-Holland.

BAGOZZI, R. P. (1981) "An examination of the validity of two models of attitude." Multivariate Behavioral Research 16: 323-359.

BENTLER, P. M. (1980) "Multivariate analysis with latent variables: causal modeling." Annual Review of Psychology 31: 419-456.

——— (1976) "Multistructure statistical model applied to factor analysis." Multivariate Behavioral Research 11: 3-25.

——— D. G. BONETT (1980) "Significance tests and goodness-of-fit in the analysis of covariance structures." Psychological Bulletin 88: 588-606.

BENTLER, P. M. and D. G. WEEKS (1979) "Interrelations among models for the analysis of moment structures." Multivariate Behavioral Research 14: 169-185.

BIELBY, W. T., R. M. HAUSER and D. L. FEATHERMAN (1977) "Response errors of nonblack males in models of the stratification process." Journal of the American Statistical Association 72: 723-735.

BLAU, P. and O. D. DUNCAN (1967) American Occupational Structure. New York: John Wiley.

BOCK, R. D. and R. E. BARGMANN (1966) "Analysis of covariance structures." Psychometrika 31: 507-534.

BOOMSMA, A. (1982) "The robustness of LISREL against small sample sizes in factor analysis models," pp. 149-173 in H. Wold and K. Jöreskog (eds.) Systems Under Indirect Observation. New York: Elsevier North-Holland.

BROWNE, M. W. (1974) "Generalized least-squares estimators in the analysis of covariance structures." South African Statistical Journal 8: 1-24.

BYNNER, J. (1981) "Use of LISREL in the solution to a higher-order factor problem in a study of adolescent self-images." Quality and Quantity 15: 523-540.

DALTON, R. J. (1982) "The pathways of parental socialization." American Politics Quarterly 10: 139-157.

DUNCAN, O. D. (1975) Introduction to Structural Equation Models. New York: Academic.

——— A. O. HALLER, and A. PORTES (1971) "Peer influences on aspirations: a reinterpretation," pp. 219-244 in H. M. Blalock, Jr. (ed.) Causal Models in the Social Sciences. Chicago: Aldine.

FISHER, F. M. (1966) The Identification Problem in Econometrics. New York: McGraw-Hill.

FOX, J. (1980) "Effect analysis in structural equation models." Sociological Methods and Research 9: 3-28.

GOLDBERGER, A. S. (1971) "Econometrics and psychometrics: a survey of communalities." Psychometrika 36: 83-107.

——— O. D. DUNCAN (1973) Structural Equation Models in the Social Sciences. New York: Seminar.

GRAFF, J. and P. SCHMIDT (1982) "A general model for decomposition of effects," pp. 197-223 in H. Wold and K. Jöreskog (eds.) Systems Under Indirect Observation. New York: Elsevier North-Holland.

GUILFORD, J. P. and B. FRUCHTER (1978) Fundamental Statistics in Psychology and Education. New York: McGraw-Hill.

HANUSHEK, E. A. and J. E. JACKSON (1977) Statistical Methods for Social Scientists. New York: Academic.

JÖRESKOG, K. G. (1978) "Statistical analysis of covariance and correlation matrices." Psychometrika 43: 443-477.

——— (1974) "Analyzing psychological data by structural analysis of covariance matrices," pp. 1-54 in R. C. Atkinson et al. (eds.) Contemporary Developments in Mathematical Psychology, vol. 2. San Francisco: Freeman.

——— (1973) "A general method for estimating a linear structural equation system," pp. 85-112 in A. S. Goldberger and O. D. Duncan (eds.) Structural Equation Models in the Social Sciences. New York: Seminar.

——— A. S. GOLDBERGER (1972) "Factor analysis by generalized least squares." Psychometrika 37: 243-260.

JÖRESKOG, K. G. and D. SÖRBOM (1981) LISREL V. User's Guide. Chicago: National Educational Resources.

——— (1978) LISREL IV. User's Guide. Chicago: National Educational Resources.

——— (1976) LISREL III: Estimation of Linear Structural Equation Systems by Maximum Likelihood Methods. User's Guide. Chicago: International Educational Services.

JÖRESKOG, K. G. and M. van THILLO (1973) LISREL: A General Computer Program for Estimating a Linear Structural Equation System Involving Multiple Indicators of Unmeasured Variables. Research report 73-5. Department of Statistics, Uppsala University, Uppsala Sweden.

——— M. van Thillo (1972) LISREL: A General Computer Program for Estimating a Linear Structural Equation System Involving Multiple Indicators of Unmeasured Variables. Princeton, NJ: Educational Testing Service.

JUDD, C. M. and M. A. MILBURN (1980) "The structure of attitude systems in the general public." American Sociological Review 45: 627-643.

KENNY, D. A. (1979) Correlation and Causality. New York: John Wiley.

KEESLING, W. (1972) "Maximum likelihood approaches to causal flow analysis." Ph.D. dissertation University of Chicago.

KESSLER, R. C. and D. F. GREENBERG (1981) Linear Panel Analysis. New York: Academic.

KMENTA, J. (1971) Elements of Econometrics. New York: Macmillan.

KREHBIEL, K. and R. G. NIEMI (1982) "A new specification and test of the structuring principle." Paper delivered at the annual meeting of the American Political Science Association.

LEE, S. Y. (1977) "Some algorithms for covariance structure analysis." Ph.D. dissertation. University of California, Los Angeles.

LONG, J. S. (1981) "Estimation and hypothesis testing in linear models containing measurement error," pp. 209-256 in P. V. Marsden (ed.) Linear Models in Social Research. Beverly Hills, CA: Sage.

McDONALD, R. P. (1980) "A simple comprehensive model for the analysis of covariance structures: some remarks on applications." British Journal of Mathematical and Statistical Psychology 33: 161-183.

McDONALD, R. P. (1978) "A simple comprehensive model for the analysis of covariance structures." British Journal of Mathematical and Statistical Psychology 31: 59-72.

MAGIDSON, J. (1977) "Toward a causal model approach for adjusting for preexisting differences in the nonequivalent control group situation: general alternative to ANCOVA. Evaluation Quarterly 1: 399-419.

MALINVAUD, E. (1970) Statistical Methods of Econometrics. New York: Elsevier North-Holland.

SCHOENBERG, R. (1982) MILS: A Computer Program to Estimate the Parameters of Multiple Indicator Linear Structural Models. Bethesda, MD: National Institutes of Health.

SÖRBOM, D. (1982) "Structural equation models with structured means," pp. 183-195 in H. Wold and K. Jöreskog (eds.) Systems under Indirect Observation. New York: Elsevier North-Holland.

——— (1975) "Detection of correlated errors in longitudinal data." British Journal of Mathematical and Statistical Psychology 28: 138-151.

SULLIVAN, J. L. and S. FELDMAN (1979) Multiple Indicators. Beverly Hills, CA: Sage.

THEIL, H. (1971) Principles of Econometrics. New York: John Wiley.

WHEATON, B. (1978) "The sociogenesis of psychological disorder." American Sociological Review 43: 383-403.

——— B. MÚTHEN, D. ALWIN, and G. SUMMERS (1977) "Assessing reliability and stability in panel models," pp. 84-136 in D. R. Heise (ed.) Sociological Methodology, 1977. San Francisco: Jossey-Bass.

WILEY, D. E. (1973) "The identification problem for structural equation models with unmeasured variables," pp. 69-83 in A. S. Goldberger and O. D. Duncan (eds.) Structural Equation Models in the Social Sciences. New York: Seminar.

WONNACOTT, R. J. and T. H. WONNACOTT (1979) Econometrics. New York: John Wiley.

WONNACOTT, R. H. and R. J. WONNACOTT (1981) Regression: A Second Course in Statistics. New York: John Wiley.

J. SCOTT LONG is Associate Professor of Sociology at Washington State University. His recent publications, focusing on issues of scientific productivity and academic careers, have appeared in American Sociological Review, Social Studies of Science, *and* Sociological Methods and Research, *among others. He is the author of a companion volume to this University Paper:* Confirmatory Factor Analysis: A Preface to LISREL.